The
Light of Egypt

or

The Science of the Soul and the Stars

VOLUME II

BY

THOMAS H. BURGOYNE

Zanoni, ♄

"Write the things which thou hast seen, and the things which are, and the things which shall be hereafter; THE MYSTERY OF THE SEVEN STARS, which thou sawest in my right hand."

Revelations, Chap. I, 19 and 20.

H. O. WAGNER
P. O. Box 20333 Montclair Station
Denver 20, Colorado.

The first edition of The Light of Egypt, Volume II, was copyrighted in 1900 by Henry Wagner M.D. and published by the Astro Philosophical Publishing Company of Denver, Colorado. The 1963 edition is a reprint of the first edition which has been out of print for many years. This book is a reprint of the 1963 edition together with additional material taken from original manuscripts of Hermetic Teachers.

H. O. Wagner.

The Light of Egypt: Vol Two
ISBN 1-58509-052-2

© 1999
THE BOOK TREE
All Rights Reserved

Dedication

———

To the Budding Spirituality of the Occident and
The Rising Genius of the Western Race,
This work is respectfully dedicated,
By the Author

FOREWARD

This is not a book about Egypt as much as it is about the search for spiritual truth. According to the author the methods used in the book date back to ancient Egypt and Chaldea—but after that, little else is mentioned directly about these ancient cultures.

It is clear that the author, Thomas H. Burgoyne, is well-schooled in wisdom from around the world, often referring to Hermetic, Kabalistic, Theosophical, and Buddhist principles. This book is divided into two parts: "The Science of the Soul" and "The Science of the Stars," which is consistent with the saying, "As above, so below." What is above in the stars is reflected below, into the human soul, as many believe.

Volume Two continues right where Volume One left off—within the areas of the zodiac and astro-theology. This is advanced information, written at a slightly higher level than Volume One.

This book is brimming with more good information on astrology than any other you are likely to see. The remaining information within this book qualifies it as being a small "occult library" in itself. There are those in the past who have used this set of books as a text for esoteric knowledge, whether they were alone or as part of a larger group. The books contain spiritual truths not easily found elsewhere, mostly concerned with man's place in the universe, both here in the world and after one dies.

The author himself, Thomas H. Burgoyne, died before Volume Two was published. It was decided to make Volume Two available because his friends and close associates were using the text for their own spiritual search and found it to be incredibly valuable. Volume One would not be complete without it.

While he was alive Burgoyne refused to be acknowledged as the author of these books. He felt the information was more important than his own ego—so that the books would be judged on their own merits rather than being judged by any personal views or biases one might have about the author. Attaching anything to the books other than the information itself, he believed, would only serve as a distraction. Only after his passing was he made known as the author. Any time he came close to being recognized as a spiritual leader, he would humbly back away and point to the knowledge rather than himself. He had many friends who never knew that he had written these books, since he was unwilling to thrust any ideas upon people who were not ready for them. This was truly a great man, with great wisdom. The best way we can thank him, and I'm sure he would have agreed, is to glean as much wisdom from these books as we can. That is all he had ever asked for.

Paul Tice

CONTENTS

The Science of the Soul and the Stars

VOLUME II

PREFACE

These lessons were issued to a few of my pupils as "Private Studies in Occultism," several years ago. The time has now come to give them to the world as a companion to the first volume of "The Light of Egypt."

It is the duty of Occult students to familiarize themselves with the subjects herein discussed. They should know the ideas of our ancestors regarding them and be familiar with their thought, in order to appreciate the sublime wisdom and knowledge of Nature as taught by them, otherwise we are sure to do them, as well as ourselves, great injustice. The history of Occultism bears out the fact that there is very little that is new to the present time.

The arrangement and classification of thought differs during each cycle of time on the different spirals, and, like the fruitage on lower rounds of Nature's progressive wheel of destiny, variety and quality are diverse, so, likewise, do we find the mental manifestations. This age, however, is blessed with a great variety and abundance of thought, in clear-cut language, that should enlighten the races of the Earth with Mother Nature's modus operandi in every department of human thought.

We hope these chapters will aid to this end, and doubtless many students will find in them the key to unlock the mysteries veiled in symbol and hieroglyphic by ancient writers. The author's object has been to make plain and easy of understanding these subjects. Much, however, has been left for private study and research, for many large volumes might be filled if a detailed description of each subject were entered upon, which task is left for those who feel so inclined. A rich reward is in store for those spiritual investigators who will follow out the paths and lines herein mapped out on Spiritual Astrology, Alchemy, and other subjects. Meditation and aspiration will open up hidden treasures that will prove a boon to Occult students, for Astrology and Alchemy are the two grand sciences that explain the why and reasons for what we see and experience on every plane of life. In this age there should be no concealing of these Divine truths. We cannot hide anything in the air, and for this reason the Sun in Aquarius will unearth and reveal to man all that the present cycle has to give during the Sun's passage through this airy sign.

The watery sign, Pisces, through which the Sun manifested during the past 2,160 years, gave up to man their secret powers and hidden attributes in steam as a motive power, which man has completely mastered. He will likewise master the airy forces during the present sub-cycle of the Sun in Aquarius. Already we see him using liquid air and compressed air as a motive power, which will gradually take the place of steam as the Sun gets farther into the sign, or constellation, of Aquarius. Men will become immensely wiser than they have been, and it is to be hoped they will leave the written record of their achievements in science and art to show to future races their status of mind on every subject for the edification and enlightenment of coming races.

Our ancestors were denied this great privilege. Consequently their wisdom is only symbolized to us in a way that it is difficult to read and interpret correctly, yet we who have the key to their symbols can read accurately the truth they wish to convey, which stands out clearly to all capable of understanding and interpreting symbolism and correspondence correctly. History and Nature repeat themselves in every cycle of time; therefore these forces and potentialities are natural to the sign through which the Sun manifests. We can go backward or forward through the Sun's Zodiac and read correctly the history of the hoary past, as well as the present and future, by bearing in mind the sign and cycle in manifestation at any given period. When the proper time arrives, a work will be given to the world to prove to mankind the law of cycles.

God is present in all ages and races, manifesting His love and wisdom throughout infinite creations, and that He records, in His own way, the most detailed record of any event which takes place, thus giving to man a complete history of His works and will, for man's enlightenment, so that he, too, may cooperate intelligently with his God in every way that intelligence wills to manifest. Prehistoric history is not blotted out from Nature's laboratory. The Astral Book of Karmic evolution will one day reveal its hidden treasures to a waiting world in such a manner as to surprise and enlighten mankind as the recording angels give up those gems of truth they have so jealously guarded for untold cycles of time, simply because the time was not ripe for its divulgence.

There is a time for everything, and when that time arrives all past history of our planet's evolution will be written in an intelligent manner for the illumination and education of man as the masterpiece of the Living God. In this way man will worship Deity and perfect his God-nature, even to Angel-hood.

If this volume of "The Light of Egypt" meets with the same appreciation that was accorded the first volume, which has passed through four editions, and is still growing in favor every day (besides being translated into the French), the author will feel that his efforts have not been wasted, and he trusts the race will have been made better for having read his writings.

As this is his posthumous contribution to the world, the author wishes, in this connection, to pay a debt of gratitude and grateful recognition to his esteemed pupil and friend, Dr. Henry Wagner, who has so generously published nearly all of his writings. Without his aid and assistance we would not have been able, of ourselves, to have given these works to the world. Therefore, honor to whom honor is due.

Mrs. Belle M. Wagner has been chosen by the Masters as my spiritual successor and representative of the Hermetic Brotherhood of Luxor, and thus perpetuate the chain of outward connection between those in the realm of the higher life with those upon the outward plane.

She is our choice, and a most worthy one to take my place.

I make this statement in this connection for the benefit of my pupils and Hermetic students generally, as I am being personated by frauds and imposters, claiming to be Zanoni. *Verbam sap.*

It is my request that a fac-simile of my signature and symbol accompany this preface.

Dictated by the author from the subjective plane of life (to which he ascended several years ago) through the law of mental transfer, well known to all Occultists, he is enabled again to speak with those who are still upon the objective plane of life.

The additions found in this volume, not in the original manuscripts, have been supplied in this manner. The two planes of life, the objective and subjective, are scientific facts, no longer disputed by well-informed minds, and the exchange of thought will become almost universal among educated minds during the present cycle. Hence great progress will come to the Earth during the next 2,160 years, while the Sun manifests his glorious influence through the symbol of the Man.

Thanking each and all who have aided in any way to give my writings to the world, I am, in love and fraternal greetings, ever yours. *Omnia Vincit Veritas.*

Very Truly
T. H. Burgoyne. ᵴᴸ.

INTRODUCTION TO VOL. II

What study is more sublime, inspiring and profitable, in the highest sense, than the "language of the stars"—those silent monitors of the midnight sky, who reveal *His Will* as secondary causes in the administration of universal law? The science of the stars is the Divine parent of all science.

The more earnest our study, the more recondite our research and thorough our investigation of the "Science of the Stars," the more fully shall we realize the truth of the teacher's words: "Astrology is the key that opens the door to all occult knowledge." It is the key that unlocks the mysteries of man's being; his why, whence, whither. Within the temple of Urania lies concealed the mystery of life. The indices are there, written by the finger of the Infinite in the heavens above.

It is our privilege to make this language our own, and it should be the earnest work of every true student of Nature to acquire a right understanding and correct interpretation of these Divine symbols. And, as thorough students of any language seek out the derivation of words and expressions, search for the root, or stem word, and its origin, so should the student of astrology, by sincere desire and earnest study, seek to know the origin and root of these starry words and complex expressions of the "language of the stars."

The Sun, Moon and five planets° of our solar system are to us symbols of the reflected and refracted rays of the triune attributes of the great Central, Spiritual Sun: Life, Light and Love, analogous to the three primary colors in Nature, which become still further refracted into four secondary or complementary colors, rays or attributes, the seven constituting the active principles of Nature, the seven rays of the solar spectrum, the seven notes of a perfect musical scale, there being throughout a perfect correspondence, and all are but different modes of vibration or activities of the Supreme Intelligence.

And, as we know, the seven rays of color reflect an almost infinite variety of tints, that, octave upon octave, are built upon the seven natural tones in music, so, also, are these seven active principles divided and subdivided into innumerable forms, qualities and mani-

---

° Uranus and Neptune belonging to a higher octave.

festations of the first trinity—Life, Light, Love, life being the manifestation of the second two, love and wisdom, which in turn are the dual expressions of the "One."

Upon the knowledge of these Divine truths Pythagoras built the theory of the "music of the spheres." Let us pause and listen to this celestial music.

Suns and their systems of planets sound forth the deep bass tones and rich tenor, while angelic races take the silvery treble of the Divine melody, octave upon octave, by more and ever more ethereal system upon system, to the very throne of Deity—the Infinite, Eternal source of Light, Life and Love. Let us learn, through the knowledge of the stars, to attune our souls to vibrate to the Divine harmony, so that we may take our places in the celestial choir and blend our voices with those of the celestial singers, chanting the Divine anthem: "We Praise Thee, O God!"

To resume. If we would gain a correct knowledge of astral science we should study astrology in its universal application, side by side with its more intricate phase and the details, as manifested upon the individual man and his material destiny.

Let us digress for a moment. The intellectual minds, the material scientists, who cavil at the "science of the stars," declaring it to be mere fortune-telling, consequently false, do but air their ignorance of this most profound subject, not knowing that it embraces and contains all sciences, all religions, that have ever been or ever will be, comprises all history of every age, of races, empires and nations; that it is the only true chronology, and marks the destiny, not only of personal man on every plane, but of the human family as a whole. All mythologies find their explanation in this starry language, and every religion is founded upon the movements of our solar system. The rise and fall of empires and races of men are written in its pages.

To master as far as we are capable, and our limited space of life here will permit, we must pursue the study in its broad sense, as already stated, in the external application of the starry influx and upon the interior planes of action from God to the mineral, the mineral to man; aye, and man to the angel, finding in every section a complete and perfect correspondence.

To master the alphabet should be the first step, whose vowels, diphthongs and consonants are the planets and shining Zodiac. It is very essential to clearly comprehend the action and reaction of the planets upon the human organism, as an integral part of the universal organism; ever remembering that the starry vowels, in combination with the consonants, or Zodiac, form the infinite expressions comprising the language of the starry heavens in their threefold manifestation upon the external planes of life; while the radiant constellations are the ideas which find expression through this language, which is likewise a science, accurate in its mathematical construction and perfect in geometric proportion.

The student should ever bear in mind that astrology, like every other science, is progressive. The underlying principles are always the same. These are like the "laws of the Medes and Persians," but the plane of action is constantly changing.

It is a well-established and indisputable truth that from the Sun, the solar center of our system, is derived all force, every power and variety of phenomena that manifests itself upon Mother Earth. Therefore, when we remember that the solar parent passes through one sign of his celestial Zodiac in 2,160 years, a twelfth part of his orbit of 25,920 years, we see that from each sign in turn he (the Sun) rays 'forth an influx peculiar to that special sign; and, as there are no two signs alike in nature or quality, hence the passage of the Sun from one sign into another causes a change of polarity in planetary action, which can be fully demonstrated and conclusively proven. It follows, as a natural sequence, that the rules formulated and taught by astrologers in reference to the plane of planetary influence in one sub-cycle will not hold good in the next. To illustrate: In the year 1881 the Sun passed from the sign Pisces into Aquarius, thus beginning a new cycle of solar force. The human race has entered upon a cycle in every respect differing in nature and action from the past cycle of 2,160 years. The sign Aquarius is masculine, electric, positive. It is intellectual in character, scientific, philosophic, artistic, intuitive and metaphysical. It is the sign of the Man. The truths of the past are becoming etherealized. Our solar parent has scarcely crossed the threshold of the sign Aquarius, and already we observe in many directions the activities of the peculiar influx. True, it is but the first flush of the dawn of a new era, the harbinger of a glorious day to our race. In the light of this truth, ponder well on the nature of the influx radiating from the solar center, each orb of his shining family absorbing a different ray, or attribute, of solar energy, corresponding to its own peculiar nature. The Earth, in her annual passage about her solar parent, receives the harmonious or discordant vibrations of this astral influx according to the many angles she forms to the various planets.

We see, then, that the Earth is enveloped in an atmosphere, or zone, of occult force we recognize as humane, mental, positive, etc., acting and reacting upon the human family through the laws of vibration in strict and exact ratio to its interior capacity to receive and ability to externalize upon the material plane of being. The results, as far as this stage of existence goes, will be manifest as man vibrates harmoniously or otherwise to the stellar cause.

The present sub-cycle producing an entirely different influence to that of the past cycle, whose force was watery, magnetic and feminine, causes a warring of elements, confusion and uncertainty, until the old are displaced by the new conditions. We should learn from these facts that it is folly to brand as false and condemn as worthless the rules and formulas, and even religious thought, of the past when we find upon careful investigation and crucial tests their inadequacy to account for present conditions. They were true in their cycle, and applied to past conditions and states of mental development. But in this new era, upon whose threshold we now stand, the vibrations become more intense. Man's whole nature is being tuned to a higher key. We must not forget that these cycles apply to the race in their effect, and to the individual only as an integral part of the whole. To illustrate. The sign Aquarius is an electrical, positive, masculine influence, and will consequently manifest its chief activities upon the masculine qualities of the human soul; and to-day we have evidence of this in the gradual enfranchisement of woman, arousing the positive attributes of her nature in demanding equal rights with her brother, man, in the political arena, as she has already done in the educational field. The masculine portion of the race is becoming more aggressive, mentally, asserting greater individuality, independent thought and action. The intellect of the race is being directed, however slowly, into scientific channels, while the human soul is slowly awakening to a sense of a deathless immortality and a desire for spiritual truth. It is slowly but surely shaking off the yoke of an effete priesthood and the fetters of superstition and tyranny.

Intelligent man talks of the new scientific and intellectual era that has dawned upon the world; of the necessity for a new religious system, based upon scientific truths, which can be demonstrated, combined with the pure spiritual essence found in all systems of religion; a religion with more spirituality and less theology; a broader charity and less dogma, and deeper love for God and man, its only creed.

We must now consider the astral influence of the cycle upon the physical organism of mankind, and particularly of the Western races, who are moving upon the upward arc of the cycle. It is quite evident that a radical change must take place in the physical form and constitution with the influx of more intellectual, ethereal and spiritual vibrations. The organism must become more refined and compact, a greater degree of sensitiveness be attained, with a highly nervous system. The forerunner of this superior organism is now apparent in the numerous schools of physical culture and gymnasiums throughout the land, the many articles and pamphlets on deep, rythmic breathing disseminated among the people, and last, but not least, the various schools of mental healing, etc. The masses look on and wonder, while they exclaim: "What marvelous changes are coming to the world!" but are utterly ignorant of the cause of the mysterious change. To the student of Hermetic Philosophy there is no mystery involved. He knows the cause, and confidently watches for the effect.

Each one must seek to comprehend for himself, according to the light he may receive, basing his premises upon the *true principles* of astrology, carefully noting the triune aspect of planetary influence upon humanity, ever remembering that the Sun and Moon are the great factors in human destiny, and that his premises and conclusions must occupy the same plane. Having acquired a knowledge of the science in its application to the individual, take the broader field, or universal aspect, as it applies to human races, and you will find the rise and fall of nations, empires and families marked upon the celestial dial, and in perfect accord with the influence of the Sun and planets upon Mother Earth, in her various movements. And last, but most important, seek with an earnest desire for truth to learn the relation of those glittering constellations of the shining Zodiac to the human soul and their influence in shaping its eternal destiny. This will reveal the whole of involution and evolution in a general sense.

A faithful, earnest and devout study of the "Science of the Starry Heavens" will lead us on to other planes of thought, relating to still more interior realms of knowledge than we perhaps now dream of, and, in the words of the master: "A true knowledge of the stars will include a true knowledge of the soul," and we shall realize "the mystical link that binds the soul to the stars."

MINNIE HIGGIN.

CHAPTER I

THE ZODIAC

To the ordinary astrologer the Zodiac is simply a band of space, eighteen degrees wide, in the heavens, the center of which marks out the pathway of the Sun during the space of one year of 365 days, etc.

The twelve signs are to him simply thirty degrees of the space (12 times 30 equal 360), bearing the names of the constellations which once occupied them. Nay, he, as a rule, still imagines in some sense that the signs (constellations) are still there, and that the power and potency of the twelve signs is derived from the stars which occupy the Zodiacal band of the skies.

But this is not so, as any ordinary astronomer well knows. This single fact, i.e., the gradual shifting of the constellations, the *displacement*, let us say, of the starry influx from one sign to another without any *allowance* being made in the astrologer's rules for any such change, has been one of the greatest obstructions to the popular spread of the art among *educated minds*. Argues the scientist: The "fiery influence of Aries," if depending upon the stars of that constellation, ought now to be shedding forth their caloric from the sign Pisces, and Aries ought to be lumbering along with the earthy Taurine nature. So, also, the lords of these signs ought to be changed, but that they are not can be proved by the fact that our earliest records of that dim, historic past show, equally as well as your latest "text-book," that Mars is the lord of Aries—a fiery planet in a fiery sign; but astrologers still say that Pisces is watery and Aries fiery, *which is not the case, if the stars have any influence at all.* "It is not necessary," say these logical thinkers, "to learn your abstruse science if we can demonstrate that the very basis upon which your conclusions rest is in every sense fundamentally false." The scientific facts of the case are as follows: The influence of the twelve signs, as described by astrologers, is a delusion, because in all ages they are reported the same; whereas *we know* that every 2,160 years each sign retrogrades to the extent of thirty degrees, and, as your art does not make allowance for this, it is false. For, if the influence of the twelve signs does not emanate from the stars occupying the space of those signs, it must emanate from nothing—a doctrine well suited, no doubt, to musty old sages of your superstitious

Chaldea, but quite out of court in our progressive age—the last decade of our cultured and scientific nineteenth century.

So far, so good. And so the world rolls along its bright pathway in the heavens, little heeding the logical conclusions of an exact science. But to an initiate of those inner principles of our planet's constitution all these mental conflicts have a meaning and a purpose within Nature's divine economy; for it is neither wise nor expedient that the masses, with popular science in the lead, should grasp the truths which Mother Nature reserves *alone* for her own devoted priests.

The shining Zodiac, with its myriad constellations and its perfect galaxy of starry systems, derives its subtle influence, as impressed astrologically upon the human constitution, from the solar center of our solar system, NOT FROM THE STARS which occupy the twelve mansions of space. *Aries,* the fiery, and *Pisces,* the watery, *are always there,* and, instead of its being an argument against astrology, it is one of its grandest truths that, in all ages and in all times, Aries, the first sign of the Zodiac has been found *ever the same,* equally as well as Pisces the last.

In order to convey our meaning, let us digress for a moment and bring forth a fitting illustration. The condition of our atmosphere and the surrounding objects—vegetation, etc.—have a peculiar condition and a magnetism wholly their own when surveyed exactly at sunrise. There is a freshness and peculiar sense of buoyancy not visible at any other time. If this state could be registered by any instrument and compared with any other set periods during the day, it would offer a remarkable contrast. Two hours later there is a very different influence, and at noon there is a wonderful contrast. The same may be said of sunset, and again at midnight; and, lastly, note the difference two hours before dawn. This is the coolest period of the whole twenty-four hours. These are facts, and yet our hearts are all beating to the same life-flow, and the Earth is no farther away from the parent Sun; and yet it is the angle at which we, THE INHABITANTS, receive this Sun's light that makes all the difference between dawn and sunset, noon and midnight.

When to these facts it is further added that it is sunrise, noon, sunset and midnight at the same instant, all the time, to some of the various, different portions of the globe, it demonstrates most conclusively that the Earth itself is enveloped, so to say, in a complete circle of conditions very similar to the twelve signs of the celestial Zodiac.

If we apply the foregoing illustration to the twelve signs of the Zodiac, we shall see a perfect analogy. We shall find that when the Sun reaches the celestial equator, so that it is equal day and equal night on the Earth, that he is on the line of the celestial horizon; it is cosmic sunrise. Hence Aries, the fiery Azoth, begins his active influx, and extends for thirty degrees, equal to two hours of the natural day.

It is the fiery red streams of awakening life that we all manifest at sunrise; then comes a change of magnetic polarity after the first fiery flush of cosmic life; the gleeful chattering of the birds and the cackling of the poultry. A reaction is noted; all things before active become restful and quiet.

So it is with vegetation, so it is with infant life, and so it is with cosmic conditions.

This corresponds with the sign Taurus. It is the solar influx, thirty degrees removed from his point of equilibrium toward the North. As this sign represents the powers of absorption, we see that at this period vegetable and animal life is quietly absorbing, for its own use, the fiery streams of solar life.

Again we view the activity of solar influx from a different angle and change of polarity, and all things become active. It is executive force. This corresponds to the sign Gemini. It is the solar influx, sixty degrees removed from his point of equilibrium. Then comes another change of magnetic polarity. It is rest from labor; it is noon.

This corresponds to Cancer. The analogy is perfect. It is the solar influx, ninety degrees removed from his point of equilibrium toward the North, and the highest point in the arc of his apparent journey and of cosmic life. It is the equilibrium of life forces.

Again the fiery influx begins its activity, and, as the hottest part of the day is about two hours after noon, or middle of the day, so is solar influx most potent at this point in the Zodiac.

This corresponds to the sign Leo. It is the solar influx, removed 120 degrees from his point of equilibrium and thirty degrees toward the South. And so on month after month, until the last one, Pisces, which well corresponds to the watery skies of February and the lifeless period two hours before dawn of a new day upon the Earth, a new year to man and a new cycle in the starry heavens. The Zodiac, then, as it applies to the human constitution and the science of astrology, has its foundation in the Sun, the center and source of life to the planet; and the twelve signs are the twelve great spaces of our Earth's annual orbit about her solar parent, each one typical of its month, and each month typical of its corresponding action upon our Earthy conditions.

As each sunrise is different in its aspects, so are no two signs of the Zodiac alike. The sunrise on the first of March is wholly different from the sunrise upon the first of May. So is the beginning and ending of each sign, and the beginning and ending of each natural day, peculiar unto itself.

When we reflect upon the inner laws of this action and inter-action, we come nearer and nearer to the one great occult fact, viz.: *The Divine Oneness of life.*

We find a perfect analogy between the destiny, the life, and ex-pression of life on the Earth, and the life and material destiny of embodied man. He, too, has his sunrise, the beginning of a new day of life, the seedtime, the flowering season, when life wears a roseate hue; the ripening fruits of experience, his harvest-time—it may be tares or golden grain; his gradual decay, the ebbing of the life forces and the icy winter of death; his gentle zephyrs and destructive hurricanes, floods and tempests, periods of drought and plenty. Within his triune constitution there are spring tides and low tides of physical, intellectual and spiritual forces. Man also makes the annual journey about the solar center, when, at the beginning of each new year to him, the life forces of his soul are renewed, regalvanized, so to say, according to the magnetic polarity of his constitution.

And so, every form of life has its Zodiac, its orbit of life and destiny. It may be infinitesimal, or vast beyond conception, each in its own peculiar plane. So we see that, the whole visible universe is one vast organism, the medium of expression for the invisible, real universe— the soul and God, the great central Sun, the eternal center of all life, binding the whole into unity—*one life.*

The celestial signs of the shining Zodiac have no existence to us apart from the graceful and unwearying motion of our Mother Earth. She alone makes our seasons, years and destiny; and she alone, by her motion about the Sun, determines the thrones and mansions of the planetary powers.

The astrological Zodiac of a Saturn or a Mars cannot be like ours. Their years and seasons are peculiar to themselves and their material conditions; hence the twelve constellations have no existence as objective facts of concrete formation or cosmic potentiality. No! But as unalterable symbols of occult truth, the starry pictures of the shining constellations have an eternal verity. They pertain to the living realities of the human soul and its varied experience.

What the mysteries are, and what connection they have with the twelve constellations, will form the subject of our next chapter.

CHAPTER II

THE CONSTELLATIONS

The twelve great constellations of the zodiacal belt which forms the Earth's orbit and the Sun's shining pathway around the celestial universe have been considered as mere imaginary figures, or emblems, invented by an early, primitive people to distinguish the monthly progress of the Sun and mark out, in a convenient manner, the twelve great divisions, or spaces, of the solar year. To this end, *it is thought,* the various star groups, termed constellations, were fancifully imagined to represent the various physical aspects of the month, under, or into, which they were consecrated by the Sun's passage during the annual journey, so that, in some sense, the twelve signs, or constellations, were symbolical, not only of the seasons, but also of the labors of the year.

That such a system seems perfectly natural to the learned mythologist, and that granting the ancients so much is a very great concession toward this *childish knowledge* is, of course, quite excusable when we are constantly told, or reminded, that actual science—that is to say, *"exact science,"* does not date backward more than a couple of centuries at most.

Even the modern astrologer, much as he descants upon the influence of the twelve signs, has but little, if any, real knowledge of this matter above and beyond the purely physical symbolism above mentioned. And perhaps it is as well that such a benighted condition prevails, and that the Divine, heavenly goddess is unsought and comparatively unknown. The celestial Urania, at least, in such isolation remains pure and undefiled. She is free from the desecrating influence of polluted minds.

Such, in brief outline, is the general conception of mankind regarding the shining constellations that bedeck, like fiery jewels, their Maker's crown, and illumine with their celestial splendor the wondrous canopy of our midnight skies. Is there no more than a symbol of rural work in the bright radiance of the starry Andromeda, the harbinger of gentle spring? Nothing, think you, but the fruit harvest and the vintage is in the fiery, flushing luster of Antares and the ominous Scorpion? Are men so spiritually blind that they can perceive nothing but the symbol of maturing vegetation and the long summer's day in the glorious splendor of Castor and his starry mate and brother, Pollux?

It would, indeed, seem so, so dead is the heart and callous the spiritual understanding of our own benighted day. To the initiate of Urania's mysteries, however, these dead, symbolic pictures become endowed with life; these emblems of rural labor or rustic art transform themselves from the hard, chrysolitic shell and expand into the fully developed spiritual flowers of spiritual entities, revealing in their bright, radiating lines the awful mystery of the soul's genesis, its evolution and eternal progressive destiny amid the mighty, inconceivable creations yet to come; pointing out each step and cycle in the soul's involution from its differentiation as a pure spiritual entity, a ray of Divine intelligence, to the crystallization of its spiritual forces in the realms of matter and its evolution of progressive life; the same eternal symbols of the springtime, the glorious summer, the autumn and winter of its eternal being.

In making this attempt, probably the very first within the era, to convey in plain and undisguised terms the interior mysteries of the twelve constellations, the reader and student is advised to ponder deeply upon the outlines presented. The subject is too vast to present in one or two chapters. Therefore we hope that this revelation may incite the student to further research. The real significance, the true, spiritual importance of such mysteries, can only be realized and fully appreciated after prolonged meditation and careful study.

With this brief digression, which we consider needed advice, we will resume our task, and attempt to usher our student into the weird labyrinth of Solomon's starry temple—"the house not made with hands, eternal in the heavens."

I. Aries ♈

"First Aries, in his golden wool."

This constellation represents the first Divine idea, the "word" of the Kabbalist, and the first active manifestation of the glorious En Soph. In other words, it is *mind in action,* the first pulsation of Deity in the dual aspects of "Lord and Creator." To the human soul it is, and always typifies, the unknown, invisible power which we term *intelligence; that which knows,* and gives unto each Deific atom of life that distinguishing, universal, yet deathless force which not only constitutes its spiritual identity and physical individuality, but enables it to pronounce, in the presence of its Creator, those mystic words: "I am that I am." In other words, this beautiful constellation symbolizes the first pulsation of that ray of pure intelligence which constitutes the Divine Ego of the human soul. It is the force that impels ever onward the life atom in its evolutionary progress, and reveals to us the beginning, or first manifestation, of the Divine Ego as an active, self-existing atom of Infinite spirit, within angelic spheres.

Seeing the actual, spiritual reality symbolized in Aries, how easy it is to note its full significance upon the external plane when refracted and reflected into the planes below through the complex action of the human organism, conveying the same radical influx in the first astrological month and the first sign of the Zodiac. We can read a perfect parallel in the astral influx upon the human body, as set forth in the "Light of Egypt," Vol. I, which says Aries symbolizes the sacrifice and represents the springtime, the beginning of a new year. The first action of pure intelligence brought forth the first expression of form, and led to the sacrifice of its angelic state, and, having gained the victory over the lower realms of matter, once more the springtime of a new life, with the promise of life, light and love.

The sign Aries represents the thinking powers of humanity; in short, the active, intellectual being, the lord of material creation—Man; and in its cosmic relations, as shown under "The Occult Application of the Twelve Signs" (Vol. I), we find the same perfect analogy.

II.   Taurus ♉

"He (Aries) turns and wonders at the mighty Bull (Taurus)."

The second constellation of the shining twelve represents the first reaction of spiritual conception. In other words, it is the mind's attention to its own ideas. In the Kabbalah it represents that peculiar state of executive force whereof it is symbolically said: "And the Lord saw that it was good," after each act of creation.

When intelligence first manifests itself form is a matter of necessity, and, as no form can possibly exist without matter, so Taurus is the first emanation of matter in its most etherealized state. Hence it is feminine, Venus the ruler thereof, and it represents the first pure form of the human soul, as it existed in its bright paradise within the angelic spheres of its parents, and reveals to us the first surprise of intelligence in embryo, the first sensation of consciousness, so to say—conscious of its Divine selfhood. Hence "He (the male spirit of pure fire, Aries), glorious in his golden (solar) wool, turns (expressing reaction) and wonders at the mighty bull (or material form)." Thus the first idea of pure intelligence in embryo, the result of action in Aries, becomes objective to its consciousness and is surprised at its own conception. It is the first sensation of pure, Divine love within angelic realms, and it (the male spirit of pure fire) sees that it is good.

Bringing this spiritual reality within our conception, and comparing it with its reflected astrological influx, what a beautiful harmony we find, and yet so simple that verily we cannot refrain from once more quoting our old-time, worn, yet, nevertheless, golden law: *"As it is above, so it is below; as on the Earth, so in the sky."* Reflecting that Taurus is an Earthy sign, and a symbol of servitude, we see that matter is ever the servant of spirit, a necessary means for the manifestation of intelligence, again recognized in the fecundating forces of this astrological sign on every plane of its action. And it is ruled by Venus, the love element in Nature, her sympathies ever finding expression in this beautiful sign. What can be clearer, more understandable, than, that the involved principles and Deific attributes, as represented by the shining constellations, when refracted through the human organism, so complex in its constitution, reflects qualities which are the external and parallel expression of the subjective principles, and, further, that form is absolutely necessary for the manifestation of intelligence?

III.   Gemini ♊

"He (Taurus) bending lies with threatening head, and calls the Twins
(Gemini) to rise. They clasp for fear and mutually embrace."

This bright constellation (Castor and Pollux), Gemini, is spiritually representative of the second spiritual action. Hence it is, of course, a masculine sign and positive. We have witnessed act I of the soul's drama, and, as some have said, tragedy, and in this, the third of the shining twelve, we find the opening scene of act II, viz: The evolution of the twin souls, or, more correctly, the differentiation of the Divine soul into its two natural component parts—male and female.

Here we approach one of the most arcane secrets within the wide scope of Occult philosophy, hence must be exact, and at the same time clear, in our statements. Note, then, that after the male spirit of pure, ethereal, divine fire (Aries) had conceived the first idea, and Taurus, the material envelope, had given that idea objective existence to its (the Ego's) consciousness, we find *sensation as the result.* No sooner sensation than aspiration; i.e., longing. This closes the action and the reaction.

Ever, in obedience to the unsatisfied wants of an immortal soul Nature immediately responds. Hence "He bending lies with threatening head, (that is demanding)," and calls the twins (the twin souls) to rise (to appear or evolve forth)," and as a first rude shock caused by their separation, or, rather, by their separate existence as two distinct, yet mutually dependent, forces, we have the context.

"They clasp for fear and mutually embrace."

This most impressive scene in the soul's drama is one of profound interest and sublime beauty.

In the Kabbalah we find the same parallel, wherein it is stated: "And so God created man in His own image (the action of Aries and Taurus); in His own image (mind) created He him, male and female created He them." In other words, Aries, Taurus and Gemini are thus spoken of in pure allegory.

The mundane Bible of the Jews, like everything else esteemed sacred, finds its original and perfect expression in the great Astral Bible of the skies.

To the average student the evolution of the Twin Souls is a profound mystery, embracing, as it does, the whole of involution and evolution, seeing that this beautiful constellation represents to us the first recognition, or consciousness, of the Divine Ego of its dual forces, sensation and aspiration, called forth by the action of Aries and Taurus. How beautifully has the poet expressed this first pulsation of Divine love: "They clasp for fear," etc. Evolved by the Divine will of pure intelligence, they must ever remain as separate, yet mutually dependent, forces, positive and negative, male and female, upon whose action and reaction rest the perfect evolvement of the powers and possibilities of the One.

In order to clearly grasp the whole of these ramifications, we again invite our student's careful attention to the same sign, Gemini, in its astrological aspect, as it is representatively expressed by refraction upon the human organism. We find that this sign (the representative of the constellation always) signifies the union of reason with intuition, and that it governs the arms, hands and executive forces of man.

Surely, as we reflect upon the almost marvelous inter-relationship between things spiritual and things temporal, we must conclude, with the man Jesus, that "They have eyes but they see not, and ears, but alas they hear not."

If it were not so man would, indeed, by virtue of the latent forces within him, take the kingdom of Heaven by storm and reign supreme as enthroned king of all material forms. Man, in his blindness, has relegated intuition to obscurity; has neglected the cunning of the left hand and debauched the pure love of the divine state. Consequently, the executive forces within him are unbalanced, thus rendering him the slave of material forms, instead of being their lawful sovereign. Therefore, not until, with clean hands and pure heart, he restores intuition to her throne, united with reason, can he hope to *comprehend* the reality of this arcane mystery of the twin souls, Gemini.

IV.   Cancer ♋

"And next the Twins with an unsteady pace Bright Cancer rolls."

In this beautiful constellation we witness the reaction of Gemini, the closing scene in act II. Hence it is, of course, a feminine force we are observing. In other words, it is that period (or rather one of them) wherein the Kabbalah expresses the reaction of the En Soph, via his Creators, as "And behold the Lord saw everything that He had made, and behold it was very good."

Just so Cancer, spiritually interpreted, means equalizing, hence *harmony*, which is indeed very good as contradistinguished from chaos.

To the human soul Cancer is the period of exalted rest. It is the highest point in the arc of the Divine Soul's Angelic Cycle. From this glorious, but subjective, summit or altitude in the realm of spirit it must descend.

Restless energy and the still unsatisfied longings of its own immortal nature are the forces that bring such evolution about. Having evolved the dual forces of its divine nature, the Ego sees that it is good and rests from its labor. But as this exalted state is purely subjective, and ideal, it must of necessity, to satisfy the longing for further unfoldment and desire to know, descend into material realms and conditions. From this point begins the soul's involution downward, until the lowest point in the arc is reached, viz., Capricorn.

Refer now to the sign Cancer, and carefully study out the parallel upon its astrological planes and also under its Occult aspects, as given forth in the "Light of Egypt," Vol. I, where we read: "Cancer rules the respiratory and digestive functions of humanity, and governs the reflective organs of the brain." Note the parallel. Within subjective realms the Divine soul has inspired and assimilated all that is possible to that angelic state, and knows a period of blissful rest. But the longings of its immortal nature urge on the soul. So we see that the sign Cancer symbolizes tenacity to life; to live we must breathe and eat and assimilate upon every plane of our being. It necessarily follows that, the mentality expressed by Cancer must be susceptible to inspirational currents; to inspire is to indraw. In its application, we find that this sign symbolizes love. How beautiful the harmony and contrast of the constellation and its astrological representative.

V.   Leo ♌

"Then Leo shakes his mane."

Herein is typified the third grand spiritual action which, as we find throughout Nature, travel in pairs; hence Leo is a positive, masculine constellation.

Having attained the highest point in the super-celestial states of subjective, embryonic existence; having evolved sensation and aspiration; now, inspired by a desire for immortality, the *dual soul* of the Divine Ego is once more impelled forward; but, as all evolution works in spirals, it cannot ascend higher without first apparently descending lower; so ever onward in its eternal march. This beautiful constellation symbolizes the first action on the downward portion of the arc. It is the affinities of the heart, so to say, working from within to without.

Matter, in its more etherealized form, begins to assert its sway. The allegorical serpent of Eden is working upon the feminine portion, symbolized by the heart, and, like a magnetic tractor, the soul's affinities are drawn downward, and, as if in defiance of all responsibilities, consequences, and Karma, the soul, lion-like, "shakes his mane in the imperiousness of deathless courage."

As we read these weird allegories, written by Deity in the starry vaults of heaven, the interested soul bows in reverence and awe before that almighty power we term Providence, and the profane call God.

No man has altered these pure records of divinity; no finger has interpolated one single line. They are as beautifully clear to the soul now as they were in the very dawn of Nature's awful creation.

To the Initiate into Urania's mysteries it is unnecessary to draw a parallel between the constellation and its astrological sign. They are too clear, magnificent and impressive to escape notice. To the majority of students the resembance may not be so apparent, hence, for their benefit, we will point out a few aspects of this interesting parallel.

We read that the sign Leo is the "solar Lion of the mysteries, that, ripens with his own internal heat the fruits brought forth from the Earth by the moisture of Isis (the soul)." Just so, the Divine Ego, by its eternal energy and strength, the pure fire of intelligence, externalizes through material forms the principles involved in the downward portion of the arc, as qualities and attributes of the soul (reflected in the physical man as traits and qualities). Again we are told, "this sign reveals to us the ancient sacrifice and the laws of its compensation." In the imperiousness of a deathless courage, the soul defies all consequences and responsibilities. Surely, this is the supreme sacrifice, to leave its pure, Edenic state to gain knowledge, to evolve its latent forces. And from this lion of the Tribe of Judah, is born that Divine love and sympathy which ultimately redeems and purifies the soul and saves it from death in matter. The laws of its compensation are fulfilled in the prefected man.

In its intellectual aspect, we learn that the mental forces of those dominated by this sign are ever striving to attain unto some higher state. Their ideas are grand, compared with the nature of the constellation, and all that it implies. The reflection is clear, natural and beautiful. When we reflect upon this awful period in the involution of the dual souls of the Divine Ego, as symbolized by the constellation, and the grand truths represented by the astrological sign when refracted through the human organism, the reason for Leo being named the Royal Sign becomes quite plain.

VI. Virgo ♍

"And following Virgo calms his rage again."

Beautifully expressive are these lines to those who read their mystic import aright. Virgo is the reaction of the leonine force, and is, consequently, a feminine symbol.

Action and reaction are the eternal laws upon which the cosmos is founded. They constitute the inseparable affinities, attraction and repulsion, of everything within the realm of manifested being. In this mystic constellation, we see the first ideas of maternal instinct arise. This is a necessary result of the impulsive action of the heart in Leo—the reaction from a state of imperious, defiance. The heat of rage or energy and deathless courage results in the *ideas* of something to be encountered, overcome, and of self-preservation. The dual soul descends still another volve in the spiral of its celestial journey toward crystallized forms.

Virgo, the Virgin of the skies, and eternal symbol of that Divine, immaculate conception, shows wherein these forces lie. Here is conceived, in a pure, holy sense, the first instinct of love within the dual soul. It represents that awful period in the Biblical Garden of Eden, wherein the *virgin wife* stands before the tree of knowledge, of good and evil, where she is fascinated by the allurements of matter and is unconsciously becoming enveloped in the coils of the serpent. In other words, after the cosmic force had *shaken its mane* in defiance of material forces, it is the reaction of his subjective half which sees *how good* material things are; or, in other words, "and following Virgo calms his rage again." The masculine half, or positive force of the soul, yields to temptation and is soothed by the alluring prospects.

It will be noticed in this connection that pity, reflection, and compassion, are the peculiar actions of the sign Virgo in the Zodiac (not the constellation), and that astrologically it governs the bowels. This symbolism is really very beautiful when closely compared and studied. That immaculate conception of pure love of the soul for its other half, upon the astrological plane, becomes refracted and reacts as compassion and pity. Again, the soul, within subjective realms, sees how good material things are, and its refraction represents the assimilating functions of the human organism. It also reveals to us the significance of the Lord's Supper. At this stage of its journey, the Divine Ego knows for the last time that close communion with the twin soul before the crucifixion, the wine typical of the sacrifice, the bread, and the sustaining forces, of its own immortal being.

The intellectual aspect of the sign Virgo forms a perfect analogy to the constellation, and is too evident for further remarks.

VII. Libra ♎

"Then day and night are weighed in Libra's scales;
Equal awhile, at last the night prevails."

Another volve in the spiral, and we reach the grand climax of the soul's journey, within the spiritual world.

The nature of this constellation was, for ages, concealed from all but Initiates; for the reason that, it contains the most important mysteries connected with the human soul. It is the grand transition arc between the spiritual world and the astral world; in other words, between ideal conceptions and elemental forms, between the world of design and the realms of force.

One of the chief mysteries of Libra is, that, it is androgyne, or bisexual, in nature. So far the dual soul has evolved within the realms of spirituality; here it stands, in the celestial balance, between the two, giving way to temptation, takes the forbidden fruit and instantly awakes from its purely spiritual state to become surrounded by the illusions of matter. The struggle of the soul with the attracting forces of matter is very clearly expressed in the line:—

"Equal awhile, at last the night prevails."

In other words, astral and physical darkness bedim the soul's spiritual sight, and, leaving the realms of innocence and bliss, they sink into the vortex of the great astral world.

The celestial state is now forever lost as a realm of angelic innocence. It can only be regained amid trial, sorrow, suffering, and experience, and, when regained, it is as Lord and Master, not as the innocent cherub. But when, having gained or reached the equator of the upward arc of its progress, and, united once more to its missing half, gives expression to that deathless force with which it started from the opposite point, Aries: "*I am that I am;*" no longer an embryo, but being within the *universal soul* of being. Before closing this symbolic constellation, we must reveal the mystery of its *bi-sexual nature*. In the higher or first portion of the sign it is ♎, positive to some extent, and masculine. The soul is still within the Garden of Eden and pure, clad in the raiment of God, and is represented by the Chaldean statues of "The Bearded Venus," or Venus, the Angel of Libra, as a morning star, bright Lucifer. But in the latter half, after the fruit of the tree of knowledge of good and evil (positive and neg-

ative, you see) has been partaken of, bright Lucifer falls. The Sun of
the Morning, shorn of his glory, becomes the symbol of night, or
Vesper, the evening star, and the symbol is thus ♎, and the soul loses
its heavenly raiment, or spiritual consciousness, and becomes clothed
with matter, the symbol of night.

The sign Libra in the Zodiac, in its astrological aspect, is a very
external correspondence of all the foregoing.

VIII.   Scorpio ♏

*"And, longer grown, the heavier scale inclines,
And draws bright Scorpio from the winter signs."*

We now behold the gates of Paradise guarded by the *flaming
sword* which points to the four quarters of the world. This sword is,
according to Genesis, "to guard the way of the tree of life," and such,
esoterically, it really is.

The soul is no longer dual, but separated into male and female
personalities; "and behold they see that they are naked." Stripped of
their spiritual raiment, they feel the chill of matter and the lusts of an
animal nature. They need clothing, "so God made them coats of skin."
Sex is the symbolism herein typified, and the evolution of the animal
passions of procreation, of multiplication and evolution. It is the
complete entry of the soul into elemental conditions, and the flaming
sword guarding the four quarters of the Earth to the way of life are
the four great realms of the astral world; the way to physical life in
concrete forms; and the way to life eternal through the realms of
the Sylphs, Gnomes, Undines and Salamanders. They are the basis
of all matter, known as Air, Earth, Water and Fire. Here we see that,
through the evolution of sex and its accompanying desire for procreation, these blind forces of Nature find their avenue of expression.
Spiritual consciousness almost lost, and without reason, the soul becomes the prey, so to say, of these forces of the astral world, which
is the realm of design. The soul's creations must be met and van-
quished upon the upward arc of the Cycle of Progress. They guard
or oppose the way to eternal life. Here the soul, having gained the
victory, stripped forever of its earthy raiment and the lusts of the
flesh, arrayed once more in its spiritual raiment, purified and sanctified,
it will stand once more at the gates of Paradise, where, reunited with

its missing half, it will partake of the fruit of the Tree of Life and become as Gods. Astrologically the correspondence is perfect, and so thinly disguised as to need no explanation.

IX. Sagittarius ♐

"Him Centaur follows with an aiming eye,
His bow full-drawn, and ready to let fly."

Deeper and deeper sinks the soul into material forms. The evolution of sex has produced the necessary avenues for the entrance of countless forces, and the soul is now rapidly losing the last vestiges of its spiritual conscience. In other words, Sagittarius symbolizes that state of the soul wherein it is descending to its polarizing point, and is, therefore, the vortex of innumerable opposing forces, seeking expression in different forms.

"It is the bow (strength or force of the soul), FULL-drawn and ready to let fly" its arrows (of energy) in any direction that may afford proper opportunity. Here we see the expression of that deathless, fiery force, and imperious daring and courage, within more material states; the primal fire reflected from another angle.

But everything is unsettled. It is a masculine force, and restless, and is represented under the allegory of the "Tower of Babel" and the utter dispersion of the people (entities) to the four corners of the Earth, and finally becomes involved in dense matter, and its migrations are at an end on this side of the Cycle of Necessity.

Upon the astrological plane, the zodiacal sign Sagittarius rules the motive forces and the pedestrian instinct, the thighs, or basis of locomotion; hence, we see, even here, a most perfect analogy. This sign symbolizes, also, the governing forces of humanity, which see the necessity of law and order; hence government. In this expression, we find the bow (strength or force) ready to let fly its arrows of energy in any direction the opportunity may afford; when refracted upon the human organism and reflected upon the external plane, these forces manifest as the restless spirit, that ever impels onward, seeking new fields of expression, out of which develops a sense of order, restraining and training, or the governing of self and control of others. When we reflect upon these symbols of starry truths the mind bows in reverence before the wisdom that created them.

X. Capricorn ♑

"Next narrow horns the twisted Caper shows."

The Goat, and in the realms of spirit, the crystallized mineral is the reaction of the former, and shows to us death, inertia and rest; hence Kronos, or Saturn, the symbol of death, is lord of this state and condition. It is the polarizing point of the soul's evolution in matter, and therefore, forms the lowest arc in the Cycle of Necessity.

Herein we behold the soul, imprisoned within the mineral state. The fire of the flint, and the spark in the crystal, are the only avenues of its lonesome expressions. But, as the lowest point, it is also the promise of a higher, and the symbol of a higher state, and the symbol of another spiral in its endless life.

This constellation, as the symbol of inertia and death, is also the symbol of awakening life, and prepares the soul for the more perfect expression of its powers in its forthcoming upward journey. If we pause for a moment and consider the force and power necessary to evolve out of this dark, dense, mineral realm, the foregoing sentence will become clear and forcible. Hitherto, the soul has been slowly drawn down into coils of matter, imprisoned by material forces. It has penetrated the lowest depths, and can go no farther. Rest here, is to gather strength, force. Mark well the difference and parallel between Cancer and Capricorn, opposite points in the arc. Cancer is the symbol of exalted rest within angelic realms; Capricorn the symbol of rest in dense matter. From the former state the soul is impelled forward on its downward journey; from the latter state the soul awakens to the struggle for life on the upward arc; and must now give expression to the positive powers of its immortal being, which have become involved in material form; that shall make it the master, and give it the victory over death and material forces. Surely, this is truly the promise of a new day, and higher state of existence.

It will be instructive to study this by a comparison of the zodiacal sign, Capricorn, as set forth in the "Light of Egypt," Vol. I, wherein we read: "This sign signifies the knees, and represents the first principle in the trinity of locomotion, viz., the joints, bending, pliable, movable." The analogy is perfect. The soul, which has been pliant, bending to material forces, now reverses this action, and bows the knee in awe and reverence to the higher powers of its being. When refracted upon the human organism, we find that the cold, lonesome state, and weary struggle within the mineral realm, becomes love of *self*, directing its energies to the attainment of selfish ends. What could be more natural?

XI.   Aquarius ♒

"And from Aquarius' urn a flood o'erflows."

The soul, released from its crystallized cycle of matter, now rapidly evolves into states, though material, yet entirely different. Its previous arc, from Libra to Capricorn, has been amid inorganic matter. It is now rushing with lightning speed upon its weird, toilsome, upward, journey through purely organic forms, from vegetable to animal; and, as all organic forms have their primary origin in water, so does this celestial urn express the primary conception of this physical state. Further, to more fully express this, Aquarius is typical of man, as prototype of the last grand goal of the soul's future material state—in other words, the last quadrant of the four elements, viz.: Bull, Lion, Eagle, Man.

There is something exceedingly significant in all this, and the more we ponder on this spiritual allegory of the shining constellation, the more we are impressed with the divine wisdom of those early instructors of our race, who thus preserved truth in an incorruptible form.

From this weird, but beautiful constellation, we learn how the soul has progressed, finding innumerable avenues of expression of its latent forces; the manifestation of its powers in the various chemical changes, and development of functions expressed through countless forms, on the lower planes of existence. The sacrifice of its angelic innocence, the imperious defiance and deathless courage, symbolized by Leo, have obtained the victory over the lower kingdoms; which will be incorporated into his vast empire. Yet, unstable as water, it cannot excel; or, in other words, cannot rise to a higher state within this arc, of its progressive life.

We find that the astrological expression of this constellation, the sign Aquarius, governs the legs, and is the natural emblem of the changeable, moveable, migratory forces, of the body, forming a perfect parallel with its interior symbol. There is a great deal contained in this zodiacal sign worthy of deep study and reflection.

XII. Pisces ♓

"Near their loved waves cold Pisces take their seat,
With Aries join, and make the round complete."

Once more a reaction—the last scene of the soul's impersonal drama. The constellation of Pisces is the symbol of rest and expectation. The soul has now completed the first round, or rung, in the Cycle of Necessity; and its next state is that of incarnated man. It has triumphed over every sphere below, and defied, in turn, every power above, and is now within that sixth state of the embryonic soul-world that transforms all its past knowledge, sorrow, and suffering, into experience; and produces the impersonal man.

It has traveled through constellated states within matter and spirit, and, as a human soul, with reason, intuition, and responsibility, it will, in its next state, become subject to those same powers when reflected from a different plane. The twelve constellations of its soul will manifest a complete rapport with the twelve signs of solar light and power.

With this we close. The mystic sign of this constellation is ⌐⌐⌐, or completion, a seal and a sign of its past labors.

And, as we have seen, the shining constellations are the soul's progressive history from its genesis, to its appearance within embodied conditions as man; and so, by correspondence, are the twelve solar signs symbols of man and his material destiny. The foundation has been laid, the material and resources are at hand, for his kingdom is exclusive. With his own hands he must build his temple (the symbol of the perfected man), each stone accurately measured, cut, polished, and in its proper place, the proportions symmetrical, hence, harmonious; the keystone of whose arch is *Will*, its foundation love. This accomplished, he will have completed the second round of the great Cycle of Necessity.

And who, after contemplating the wondrous harmony of this beautiful system, and the complete accord of each part, can refuse to agree with the truly inspired Addison that—

"Ever moving as they shine,
The hand that made us is divine."

CHAPTER III

As a sequel to the foregoing subjects, viz., the Zodiac and constellations, we will add the spiritual interpretation of the twelve houses of an horoscope, which completes the triune expression of these celestial symbols of eternal truths.

In revealing this mystery, we would impress upon the mind of the student that the order of the Zodiac is the reverse of the external, in its spiritual application, to the twelve houses of the horoscope.

As the four cardinal signs, viz., Aries, Cancer, Libra and Capricorn, correspond to the four angles of a natal figure, it is our purpose to explain, first, the symbology of the four angles, or cardinal points; believing the whole revelation will thus become clear and forcible.

The four angles of the horoscope correspond to the four elements, the four triplicities, and the four cardinal points, or epochs, in the soul's involution from pure spirit to the crystallizing, inert, mineral state.

The first angle is the ascendant, or House of Life. It is the eastern horizon, and symbolized by Aries. Upon the interior, this first angle stands for the birth, or differentiation, of the Divine Ego, as the result of the creative action, or impulse, of the Deific mind.

The Ego rises upon the eastern horizon of celestial states, a glowing, scintillating atom of pure intelligence, an absolute, eternal Ego, rising out of the ocean of Infinite Love.

The South angle, meridian, or Tenth House, pertaining to honor, etc., is symbolized by Cancer; the highest point in the arc of the soul's involution, as a differentiated atom of Deity within angelic spheres.

Having evolved the first dual expression of its (the Ego's) self, the twin souls—Sensation and Aspiration, or Love and Wisdom, the Ego rests awhile, radiant with celestial love and wisdom, and inspiring the Divine breath of life.

Again the restless impulse of the creative purpose arouses the Ego to further action. The culminating point has been reached, and now must begin an apparent downward course toward the western horizon.

The seventh angle, or House of Marriage, etc., is represented by

Libra (the Balance), or point of equilibrium; where the two souls are still one, balanced upon the western horizon. The alluring temptations of material illusions draw the souls downward, and, divorced from their celestial state, the radiance of Divine love becomes obscured, until the twilight of consciousness of that former state is lost in the night of material conditions.

This house signifies, also, law, and open enemies, and (Libra) justice. Sex is the law. The antagonism is surely too apparent to require explanation.

The fourth angle, or Nadir, the point opposite the M. C., signifies the frozen North, and is symbolized by Capricorn, the crystallizing point in the soul's involution. It is death, inertia; that is, crystallization of the soul's spiritual forces. It is the lowest point of the arc in the monad's downward journey. It is the night, before the awakening of a new day upon a higher plane of existence.

The remaining houses are the lights and shadows that, fill out and complete the picture, upon this, the first round of the Cyclic Ladder.

The Twelfth House, symbolized by Taurus, represents the first expression of form of the human soul. It is matter in the most etherealized state. It is the trail of the serpent; the silent, secret, tenacious, negative principle; that ultimately draws the soul down into the vortices of gross matter and death.

The Eleventh, or House of Friends, whose symbol is Gemini, the Twins, expressive of the first emanation of this sublime relationship, the dual attributes, love and wisdom, closest friends. It is sensation and aspiration, which enable the spirit to attain to the exalted state indicated by the Tenth Mansion.

The Ninth Mansion of the celestial map is the House of Science, Art, Religion, Philosophy, etc., and its symbol is Leo, the Heart, with its emotions, love, and longings, and sympathies. Having evolved the twins, and inspiring the Divine breath of wisdom; glowing with Deific love, the Ego aspires to know; and all the sympathies of the soul are aroused. Dauntless and fearless, defying all opposition and consequences, It (the Ego) is ready to sacrifice this angelic state and explore the boundless Universe in pursuit of knowledge, and goes forth on its long voyage upon the ocean of Infinite, fathomless love and wisdom.

The Eighth, or House of Death and Legacies, is symbolized by Virgo, the virgin wife, standing before the "Tree of Knowledge of Good and Evil," fascinated by the flattering prospects of greater power and wisdom. Desire and sympathy draw the soul down into realms which lead to death, and the beginning of a heritage of sorrow.

The Sixth, or House of Sickness, Menials, and Sorrow, is symbolized by Scorpio. The fall, from Libra through Scorpio (sex), created the first condition of what we recognize as sickness and affliction. It is evident that this house is related to the elementals of the astral plane, which become the servitors of man.

The Fifth, or House of Children, etc., symbolized by Sagittarius, signifies the offspring of sex (Scorpio), entities sent forth to people the Earth, to take their chances of life, speculating on its future course, fearlessly eager for the struggle, gaining pleasure in its migrations and activities.

The Third House is symbolized by Aquarius. This is the first step of the upward journey, or evolution, from the inert mineral state. The changes are now rapid; the journeys innumerable; through mineral, vegetable, and animal planes, of existence. Here, the Soul Monad brings into actual practice the knowledge gained on its long voyage. The magical powers of the soul are brought into action to effect these changes in form and function, conquering material forces and planes of life, transmuting Nature's elements to its uses and purposes, and writing its history, as it journeys ever onward, step by step.

And further, this house stands in opposition to the Ninth House, symbolized by Leo; longing to expand its (the Ego's) possibilities through trial and suffering; gaining knowledge through bitter experience; yet fearlessly braving all things; guided and sustained by the imperial will of spirit. The recompense promised by that supreme sacrfice has been won in Aquarius—the Man—consecrated now to a higher existence, baptized in the waters of affliction (experience), ready to be transmuted into actual knowledge. This is Aquarius, and the Third House.

The Second House, signified as Pisces, the House of Wealth, that which has been accumulated on the long and toilsome journey— the wealth of experience, acquired through trials and struggles. And now, with higher, greater possibilities, the soul eagerly awaits the hour when it shall be born again, a conscious, responsible human being, to begin the second round of the Cyclic Ladder; on this second round, to externalize the knowledge gained, to evolve the involved attributes and forces of being,—a creature of will and intellect, to work out its destiny, as the lord of material creation.

Observe, the order of the Zodiac is reversed upon the external human plane. But, Aries is always symbolical of the first angle, and Libra of the seventh, being the point of equilibrium, while the tenth, or South, angle becomes Capricorn and the fourth Cancer. The mission of the soul now is to evolve the positive, spiritual attributes.

Aries rules the brain and the fiery, imperial will. It signifies courage, daring, etc., the first qualities necessary for the battle of life. Ruling the head, the sign and house show us the ability of man to view the field of action, to mark his chart, and arm for the war (which will be incessant); responsible for his acts, a creature of unfolding consciousness, an individual, whose measure of free will enables him to wander so far North or South of his celestial equator, within his orbit, or Zodiac.

The South angle, or Tenth House, now ruled by Capricorn, tells of the honor, position, fame, etc. (or the reverse) acquired by patient labor. The crystallized material gains, the concrete result of ambition, skill, and talent, which will, at the close of his earthly career, become liquefied by the universal resolvent; symbolized by Cancer upon the opposite angle, symbolical of the grave, the end of mundane affairs; when they will be mirrored forth in new forms in that great white sea, according to the manner in which he gained his worldly accumulations and prestige.

The seventh angle is Libra, House of Marriage; that all-important relation which may make or mar a life, the Balance is so easily disturbed in its equilibrium. To preserve its harmony, equality must reign, blending love and wisdom. It is the perfect poise of body, mind, and soul, achieved by loving obedience to the higher laws of our being and the true union of intuition and reason.

The Second House, now represented by Taurus, shows us that personal wealth and possessions must come through patient servitude, steady application, and diligence, in being able to choose and assimilate the knowledge, that will enable man to battle with material conditions, and wrest from the abundant sources of Mother Nature his share of treasure and experience. It is the battle-ground to which humanity, armed with brain and will, life and energy, goes forth to battle with material forces for the bread he must earn by the sweat of his brow, and through the silent, subtle forces of mind and soul conquer matter, thus storing up a wealth of knowledge and experience.

The Third House is ruled by Gemini, the Twins, Reason and Intuition, the brethren who aid and guide us on our many journeys in the pursuit of knowledge. As this sign governs the hands and arms and the executive forces of humanity, we see, that, the hands become the magical agents of mind, moulding into outward form the ideas conceived in the mind, projecting these into the field of active life, that he may write a bright record in the Book of Life. The hands should be kept clean, the images pure; and the perfect poise gained by the equal exercise of love and wisdom, intuition and reason, making the basis of education; the evolution of the interior or real self. This is the true meaning of this house upon the external plane. It is Occult, because it means projecting the powers of the soul into conscious life, externalizing the qualities and magical forces of spirit, as shown in the first instance by Aquarius. This can be accomplished only through pure desire and aspiration. Otherwise, the unbalanced scales, with floods and cataclysms, will be the results.

The Fifth House, ruling children, etc., is symbolized by Leo (the Heart). The joys and sorrows that offspring of every kind bring, all belong to this House of the Heart. The sacrifice indicated is too obvious for comment.

The Sixth House governs sickness, disease, etc., and its symbol is Virgo, an Earthy sign, clearly showing us that the material form is the matrix, out of which are born disease and suffering. But, the perfect assimilation of the fruit of the "Tree of Knowledge of Good and Evil;" transmuting the trials, experiences, sorrows, and suffering of the physical and external life into true wisdom; makes man master of his material universe; and the blind forces of Nature become his servants. Having accomplished the task, and attained the harmonious poise, or balance, in Libra, the individualized soul arrives at the eighth step in the journey.

The Eighth House, or House of Death and Legacies (Scorpio). The old Adam dies. The sensuous has no place in the balanced, harmonious being, but recognizes sex as the law, the door to regeneration now, and that a new legacy is awaiting him.

The Ninth House, Sagittarius, where, with the knowledge acquired, self sits in judgment upon the works of the hands and mind, whether or no they have been well done; the sacrifice of the lower nature properly made, control of the triune being established, the transmutations correct and accurate, assimilation perfect and free from dross, harmony gained by loving obedience to the higher law of being, and thus becomes ruler of his kingdom; the long journey almost accomplished, so far as Earth is concerned, perceiving and understanding that all sciences, philosophies, and religions, have their origin from one primal source. Having penetrated the depths in reverent obedience to the Divine law of creation, and evolved the attributes of the dual constitution, the forces of his being become crystallized. He has reached the culmination of his earthly pilgrimage, and stands forth the perfected human reflection of the higher self.

The Eleventh House is represented by Aquarius on the human plane. Friends surround and welcome him. These friends are the pure thoughts, noble impulses, lofty ideals, and generous deeds. The bread cast upon the Waters of Life returns to nourish and sustain him in his encounter with the secret foes, symbolized by the Twelfth House and Pisces. The idols, false ideas, and vampires of his own creation, are to be cleansed and washed away by the Waters of Love, the universal solvent that is ever seeking to bring about change and new forms; born again of water to make the round of the astral Zodiac, until, having again reached the equator of the ascending arc, where he is reunited to the missing half of his soul, the true friend of the Edenic state; the highest point in the arc of human progress won; the honor and glory of a perfected soul; the Lord and Master, the "I am that I am," to rest in peace in the heart of Infinite Love and Wisdom.

CHAPTER IV

There is one species of Divine revelation which has not, and cannot, be tampered with, one great Bible, which forms the starry original of all Bibles.

This sacred Bible is the great Astral Bible of the skies; its chapters are the twelve great signs, its pages are the innumerable glittering constellations of the heavenly vault, and its characters are the personified ideals of the radiant Sun, the silvery moon, and the shining planets, of our solar sphere.

There are three different aspects of this sacred book, and in each aspect the same characters appear, but in different roles, their dress and natural surroundings being suited to the natural play of their symbolical parts. In fact, the whole imagery may be likened unto a play, or, rather, a series of plays, performed by the same company of artists. It may be a comedy, or it may be melodrama, or it may be a tragedy; but the principles behind the scenes are ever the same, and show forth the same Divine Oneness of Nature; demonstrating the eternal axiom: *One truth, one life, one principle, and one word,* and in their fourfold expression, is the four great chapters of the celestial book of the starry heavens.

In this aspect the visible cosmos may be represented as a kaleidoscope. The visible constellations, planets, and other heavenly bodies, are the bits of colored glass; and Deity the invisible force, which keeps the instrument in motion. Each revolution produces a different pictorial figure, which, complete in its harmony of parts, is perfect in its mathematical proportions, and beautiful in its geometrical designs. And yet each creation, each form, and each combination of forms, are produced by the same little pieces of glass; and all of them, in reality, are optical illusions; i.e., natural phenomena, which deceive the physical senses. So it is with Cosmic Nature.

It must not, however, be supposed, because of this perfect and continual illusion of Nature's playful phenomena, that all visible creation is purely an illusion of the senses, as some cranky metaphysicians would have it, because this is not so.

Going back again to our kaleidoscope, we can clearly see that without it, and its tinted beads, no such optical illusion is possible. There is, then, a basis of spiritual reality to all visible physical phenomena; but this basis lies concealed, because of the perfect illusion which the reflected image produces upon the material plane of the physical senses. The beads themselves are real. These are the basis, and the different pictures are the result, not of the beads, but of the angle from which they are reflected to our earthly vision. In other words, *the plane from which we behold the phenomena.*

Hence, the nearer we approach the Divine center of our being, the less complicated Nature's original designs become, and the farther we are removed from that central source, the more weird, mysterious, complicated, and incomprehensible, does Mother Nature appear, to the finite human mind. And this is especially so, to man's theological instinct, his religiosity, that constitutes one of the fundamental factors of his being.

Nature is ever *one* in her original truths and their duplicate reflections; but ever conflicting and contradictory in her multiplied refractions through the minds of men. Therefore, we will present the primary concept of that grand Astro-Theology formulated by man's great progenitors; and view the simple machinery, by which they typified to the primitive mind a general outline of Nature's Divine providence.

All sacred books begin with an account of physical creation, the culmination of which, is the appearance of man and woman, as the parents of the race; and, while they will differ considerably in detail and make-up, the basic ideas embodied are essentially the same in all cosmo-genesis; so that in the Jewish Bible, accessible to all, one can read the primitive story of creation from a Jewish point of view, and, when read, rest satisfied that he has read the revelation vouchsafed to man in every age and in every clime. The only difference is one of mental peculiarity and national custom, along with climatic conditions. Hindoo, Chaldean, Chinese, Persian, Egyptian, Scandinavian, Druidic and ancient Mexican are all the same—different names and drapery, to suit the people only, but essentially the same in the fundamental ideas conveyed.

THE CREATION OF THE WORLD

The simple story of creation begins at midnight, when the Sun has reached the lowest point in the arc—Capricorn. All Nature then is in a state of coma in the Northern Hemisphere, it is winter time, solar light and heat are at their lowest ebb; and the various appearances of motion, etc., are the Sun's passage from Capricorn to Pisces, 60°, and from Pisces to Aries, 30°, making 90°, or one quadrant of the circle. Then begin in real earnest the creative powers, it is spring time. The six days are the six signs of the northern arc, beginning with the disruptive fires of Aries. Then, in their order, Taurus, Gemini, Cancer, Leo, Virgo; then Libra, the seventh day and the seventh sign, whose first point is opposite Aries and is the opposite point of the sphere, the point of equilibrium, equal day and equal night, it is autumn. It is the sixth sign from Aries, the first creative action, and so the sixth day following the fiery force, wherein God created the bi-sexual man. See Genesis, 1:5-27: "So God created man in His own image; in the image of God created He him, male and female created He them."

It is the seventh, or day of the Lord (man), the climax of material creation and Lord of all living things, and he rests in the blissful Garden of Eden. This seventh day and seventh sign is the concealed sacred Libra (♎), the perfect union of the sexes. Then comes the fall from Libra, through Scorpio, and banishment from the Garden of Eden. That is the victory of Satan, or Winter, over Summer, etc. It is useless to repeat the same old, old story. The yearly journey of the Sun around the constellated dial of Deity is the Astro basis of all primitive cosmology.

THE SCHEME OF REDEMPTION

In addition to the creation of the world and the fall of man through sin, we find all people in possession of a grand scheme of redemption, and, like the former, we shall find them all essentially the same. They all require a mediator between the angry God and disobedient man, and they all require that this mediator shall be Divine, or semi-Divine. Nothing less can satisfy Deity's demands; or, rather, let us say man's own carnal imagination. It is simply another turn of our cosmic kaleidoscope, and behold! the actors have changed. Capricorn becomes the stable of the Goat, in the manger of which the young Savior of the world is born. As a type of all, we will take the Gospel Savior. It is again midnight. The Sun enters the sign Capricorn on the twenty-first of December. This is the lowest point of the arc, South, and for three days he is stationary, or in darkness. And now it is Christmas Eve. He (the Sun or Savior) begins to move, and at midnight is born as the celestial Virgo is rising upon the Eastern quadrant of the skies; hence the Sun-God is born of a Virgin. Then comes the flight to escape Kronos, or Saturn (ruling Capricorn), who kills the young babes. There is a period of silence in the God's history while the Sun is in transit through the signs Capricorn and part of Aquarius. That is, he is hidden or obscured by the clouded skies of this period. We hear of him but once again until he, the Sun-God, or Savior, is thirty years old, or has transited thirty degrees of space. He has entered the sign Aquarius (symbolical of the Man.) Now begins the period of miracles.

Let us digress for a space, and refer to our chapter on the constellations. We shall find a perfect analogy between this miracle-working period and the constellations Aquarius and Pisces, as therein given. The first miracle we read of is turning water into wine. This may be seen in a threefold aspect. The Sun-God changes by his life-forces the waters of winter into the rich vintage of the harvest, where the Virgin (Virgo) Mother again appears. Again, the wine becomes the blood—the life offered up on the vernal cross to strengthen, renew and make merry with new life our Earth and its people. The devil (or winter), with his powers of darkness, is defeated and man saved. The final triumph is the crucifixion in Aries, the vernal equinox, about the twenty-first of March, quickly followed by the resurrection, or renewal of life. Then the God rises into heaven, to sit upon the throne at the summer solstice, to bless his people. We read, that, the Savior of mankind was crucified between two thieves. Very good. The equinoctial point is the dividing line between light and darkness, winter and summer. In other words, the Sun is resuming his northern arc, to replenish the Earth with his solar force and preserve his people from death in the coming winter. The life of a Buddha, a Krishna or a Christ, are all found in their completeness in the life of *Horus*; while the Father, Son and Holy Ghost are *Isis, Horus* and *Osirus*. The same trinity, under different names, are found in all nations. It is the *Sun, Moon* and *Human Soul*, which is the only true mediator of Man.

There is another version of this celestial crucifixion, wherein
the Sun-God-Savior, after the supper of the harvest in Virgo, is crucified at the autumnal equinox upon the equator. We read that he
was dying from the sixth to the ninth hours—three hours, three signs,
or from the 21st of September to the 21st of December, when he is
laid in the tomb. This is the lowest point of the Sun's journey in
the southern hemisphere, and darkness holds the balance in our northern hemisphere. The three days in the tomb are the three months,
or three signs, before the vernal equinox, or the resurrection, the rising
out of the South to bring salvation to the northern portion of our Earth.

We have now only to glance over various diverging lines of the
same cosmology and the same redemption. All these allegories typified *truths*. They all teach the Initiate the mysteries of creation, of
man's destiny and his necessary Cycle of Material Probation. Some
of the most beautiful parables may be read in this light. Abraham,
and the story of his wanderings in the deserts of Asia Minor; of Lot
and his unfaithful wife, are to be seen still written in the heavens.
Hagar and Ishmael are still there; so also are Esau and his brother
Jacob; the story of Joseph and his brethren; of Sampson and his
twelve labors. This is the same beautiful story. The Sun, shorn of
his glory, or solar force, at the autumnal equinox, stands upon the
equator between the two pillars of the temple (or light and darkness),
and pulls down the temple (or signs) into the southern hemisphere.
And behind this we have the eternal truth of the soul, when, giving
way to the allurements of matter (Delilah), the soul is shorn of its
spiritual covering, or conscience, and sinks into matter and death.
And the story of David and Goliath can be read to-day as clearly
as of yore.

They are eternal, spiritual verities of human nature, and record,
not only the history of the human race, its mutations and transmutations, but of the individual man and the suffering and delusive joys
of his material life. Aye, more! It is the record of all his past existence
and a type of his eternal destiny in the future.

Another turn of our cosmic kaleidoscope, and lo! the scene changes
—the play extended, the angles greater, caused by the revolution of
our solar parent through his celestial Zodiac. As the Sun passes out
of one sign into another, or, in other words, forms a different angle
to his own center of force, a new dispensation is born to the world;

or, rather, re-born under a new guise. The great Sun-God appears to change his nature and manifests an entirely different set of attributes. That is the way man personified this play of Nature, through his imperfect conception of the cause of this change. But to him it was, and is, a truth, and man's effort to externalize these attributes in a Divine personality was, and is, strictly from the plane of his mental development and spiritual unfoldment.

The two pictures of this Astro-Theology, as set forth in the two divisions of the Jewish Bible, will illustrate our meaning. The Sun had entered the sign Aries some time prior to the exodus from Egypt. Aries is the constellation of Mars, the fiery, destructive and warrior element, or force, in Nature, and we find the Jewish conception of God a perfect embodiment of these attributes: The Lord of Hosts, a God mighty in battle, delighting in the shedding of blood and the smell of burnt offerings, ever marshalling the people to battle and destroying their foes and the works of his own hands; a God imbued with jealousy, anger, and revenge. This was the type set up by the Jewish savior and lawgiver, Moses.

After a period of 2,160 years, we find the Christian cosmology ushered in. The Sun has entered the sign Pisces, which is ruled by Jupiter, the beneficent father. The Christ, or mediator, of the Christian Gospel was an embodiment of the joint qualities of the sign and ruling planet. Gentle, loving and merciful, His words were messages of love and peace; His work was with the poor, oppressed and fallen; he eschewed sacrifices and burnt offerings; a contrite heart was the best offering; He taught the people that God was their Father, loving all, just, yet merciful. But a strong taint of the old conception has remained with the human race, hiding, at times, the beauty of the latter concept. These are, again, the refractions of eternal truths, viewed by man from his material plane. The elements are here presented, the alphabet and its key clearly defined. Therefore, let each one explore this tangled labyrinth of Astro-Theology for him or herself, and work out the various correspondencies at leisure. It is enough to indicate the starry originals of all this seemingly confused mass of so-called Divine revelation in sacred books.

They, one and all, pertain to the same celestial phenomena, and the various Bibles are the outcome of man's serious attempt to tabulate and externalize this heavenly order, to record his conceptions of these starry aspects and movements with their corresponding effects upon the Earth.

Probably the purest system to us is that which may yet be derived from Chaldean sources. This sacerdotal caste were the most perfect in their astral conceptions and complete in their symbolic system of recording, and if the great work found in King Sargon's library in seventy tablets is ever translated, it will prove of priceless value to the student of these weird, but sublime, astrological mysteries.

In conclusion, as we reflect upon the fourfold aspect of the subject that we have presented in outline in these pages, the whole imagery passes in review before the mental vision. We see that the radiant constellations of the heavenly vault, with the beautiful reflection and counterpart, the shining Zodiac, are the two halves of the great *Cycle of Necessity*, the spiral of eternal, universal life, which binds the whole into unity, and unity into infinity. It is the grand scheme of creative life. The seven principles of Nature, or Divine Activities, are the forces producing the phenomena within seven angelic states, seven kingdoms, and, by seven planets, upon the external plane; the planets being the passive mediums of the positive spiritual forces. Upon this dual spiral, which reflects the seven rays of the solar spectrum is produced seven musical notes; one half of the spiral in sound and color being the complementary of the other half. Man, the Earth, and our solar system, are revolving, each orb in its own key, and its own peculiar ray, meeting and blending with other spirals, and the whole blending into one mighty spiral Cycle of Progressive Life, revolving around the Eternal, Infinite Ego—God, ever involving and evolving the attributes, powers and possibilities of the One great central source of Being.

It is a grand orchestra, pealing out in richest *melody* and sublime *harmony*, the grand Anthem of Creation: "We Praise Thee, O God."

CHAPTER V

The Astro-Mythological system of the ancients, though forming the last section, so to say, of the mysteries of the Divine Urania, is, perhaps, the most beautiful of its general features, and perfect in the complete fulfillment of the purpose for which it was intended, viz.:— to convey to the human mind a lesson, a moral, a truth in Nature; and last, but not the least, to serve as a basis upon which its inner aspirations and its more external faith might rest in security.

When we come to examine the deep, philosophical principles of such a wise system, we are almost astounded at the result of our researches and the wisdom of human nature displayed in formulating such perfect analogies of truth, semi-truth, and of falsehood, according to the plane occupied by the individual.

Let us take one instance, which will clearly explain all the rest, for they are built and formulated after the same model. Æneas, of Greek myths and fables, is reputed to be the son of Venus by a *mortal* father, upon the plane of reality. As that of actual *parent* and *child*, of course this is an utter falsehood. To the rural population of long, long ago, and their simple, rustic conceptions, *it was a truth.*

Why so? Because they believed it, and to them it taught the required lesson of obedience to the powers that be. But if in reality it was a falsehood, how can it become a truth by the simple addition of acceptance and belief? Because it possessed a metaphysical truth, though not a physical one, in the sense accepted.

Æneas, son of Venus, whose history is so beautifully preserved by the immortal Virgil, was (metaphysically speaking) son of the goddess, because he was, in his astral and magnetic nature, ruled and governed by Venus, born under one of her celestial signs and when she was rising upon the ascendant of the House of Life, even as Jesus Christos was born of a virgin, because Virgo was rising at His birth.

Thus Æneas was, in strict metaphysical reality, a son of Venus. Having satisfied the rural mind, which thus, unconsciously, accepts an absolute truth under a physical disguise, the metaphysical thinker, the philosopher, also accepts the same fable, knowing and realizing its more abstract truth.

But, again, we are met with the objection that such a truth is only apparently a truth; i.e., on the plane of embodied appearances, and naturally the question arises, where (if at all) is the real truth of the mythos? That truth which is beyond the mere metaphysical thinker and commonplace philosopher; the truth which the Initiates recognize—where is it? That truth lies far beyond the purview of Astro-Mythology. It is connected with the center of angelic life. Sufficient here to say that, as there are seven races of humanity, seven divisions to the human constitution, seven active principles in Nature, typified by the seven rays of the solar spectrum, so are there seven centers of angelic life, corresponding to the seven planetary forces formulated in "The Science of the Stars," and, as each one of us must of necessity belong to one of the particular angelic centers from which we originally emanated, the Initiate can see no reason why *Æneas may not in reality* belong to that celestial vortex represented by Venus upon the plane of material life. This being the case, we see how beautiful the ancients' system of temple worship must have been. The simple rustic, in reverence and awe, accepting the gross and physical meaning—the only one possible to his dark, sensuous mind. The scholar and philosopher bow their wiser heads with equal humility, accepting with equally sincere faith the more abstract form of the allegory; while on the other hand, the priest and the Initiate, lifting their loftier souls above the earth and its formulas of illusion and matter, accept that higher and more spiritual application, which renders them equally as sincere and devout as their less enlightened worshipers. It is thus we find these astro-myths true for all time, true in every age of the world, and *equally true of all nations.* And this is the real reason why we find every nation under the Sun possessing clear traditions relating to the same identical fables, under different names, which are simply questions of nationality. And when mythologists, archæologists, and philologists once recognize the one central, cardinal truth, they will cease to wonder why nations, so widely separated by time and space, possess the same basic mythology. They will then no longer attempt its explanation by impossible migrations of races, carrying the rudiments with them. They will find that this mythology was a complete science with the ancient sages, a *uni-*

versal mystery language, in which all could converse, and that it descended from the Golden Age, when there was but *one* nation on the face of the Earth, the descendants of which constituted the basic nucleus of every race which has since had an existence. In this light all is simple, clear, and easy to comprehend—all is natural.

The astronomer-priests of the hoary past, when language was figurative, and often pictorial, had recourse to a system of symbols to express abstract truths and ideas. In order to impress the minds of pupils with a true concept of the attributes of the celestial forces, we call planets, they personified their powers, qualities, and attributes. Just as the average mind of to-day cannot conceive of Deity apart from personality, so did primitive man clothe his ideas in actual forms, and in these impersonations, they combined the nature of the celestial orb with that of the zodiacal sign or signs, in which the planet exerted its chief and most potent activities. For instance, the planet Mars, whose chief constellation is Aries, was described as a great warrior, mighty in battle, fierce in anger, fearless, reckless, and destructive; while the mechanical and constructive qualities were personified as Vulcan, who forged the thunderbolts of Jove, built palaces for the gods, and made many useful and beautiful articles. Then, again, we find that Pallas Athene was the goddess of war and wisdom. She sprang from the head of Zeus. Aries rules the head, and represents intelligence. Athene overcame her brother Mars in war, which shows that intelligence is superior to brute force and reckless courage.

Here, we see three different personages employed to express the nature of the powers and phenomena produced. They were called gods and goddesses. This was quite natural, as the planets of our system are reflections of Divine principles. Esoterically, Mars symbolizes strength, victory—attributes of Deity.

Mars is said to have married Venus, teaching us that the union of skill and beauty are essential in all artistic work.

Mythology tells us that the god Mars was supposed to be the father of Romulus, the reputed founder of Rome. Romulus displayed many characteristics of the planet. The mythos is no doubt a parallel to that of Æneas. Rome was founded when the Sun in his orbit had entered the sign Aries, and Mars was the god most honored by the Romans. In time, with the degeneration of human races and their worship, to the rural mind, the subjects of the mythos became actual personalities, endowed with every human passion and godlike attribute, the former characterizing the discordant influence of the heavenly bodies upon man.

Gai, Rhea and Ceres, or Demeter (Greek), represent the triune attributes of Mother Earth. Gai signifies the Earth as a whole, Rhea the productive powers of the Earth, and Ceres utilizes and distributes the productive forces of Rhea.

In the charming story of Eros (Divine Love), son of Mars and Venus, he (Eros), we are told, brings harmony out of chaos. Here, we see the action of Aries and Taurus, ruled respectively by Mars and Venus.

The beautiful myth of Aphrodite, born of the sea foam, is Venus rising out of the waters of winter, to shine resplendent in the western skies at evening, and typifies the birth of forms, as all organic forms have their origin in water.

In all lands the Sun was known under various names, typical of solar energy, especially in reference to the equinoctial and solstitial colures.

Henry Melville, in his valuable work, "Veritas," says no reliance can be placed upon ancient dates, either of Europe, Asia, or anywhere else, and he conclusively shows that such dates are Astro-Masonic points on the celestial planisphere, the events recorded being, as it were, terrestrial reflections of the celestial symbols.

To attempt to wade through all the various systems of mythology, and explain each in its proper order, would be to write a large encyclopedia upon the subject. We have given a few examples as keys, and suggest works for study. We have here given the real key, and the student must fathom particulars for himself. The chief work, and most valuable in its line, is Ovid's "Metamorphoses." The next, also the most valuable in its line, is "The Mythological Astronomy of the Ancients," with notes (these latter are the gist and constitute the real value), by S. A. Mackey; and last, and, perhaps, in some sense, not the least, is the "Wisdom of the Ancients," by Lord Bacon. This is published in "Bacon's Essays."

A careful study of Ovid, with the key which this chapter supplies, will reveal *all* that pertains to ancient gods, demi-gods, and heroes, while a study of Mackey, and a careful comparison with "La Clef" and "La Clef Hermetique" will reveal all that pertains to cosmic cycles and astral chronology, which is the only chronology that is quite trustworthy, as far as ancient history is concerned.

While we are on this subject, we must point out some of the delusions, into which the subtle, magical teachings of the Orient would lead the student.

All the monster sphinx, half human, half animal, etc., which the ancients have preserved, are simply records of the past. They are chronological tables of cosmic time, and relate to eras of the past, of the Sun's motion, and not by any means to living creatures of ante-diluvian creations, as some wiseacres have imagined. Many of these ancient monuments, monstrous in form, are records of that awful period of floods and devastation known as the Iron Age, when there was a vertical Sun at the poles; or, in other words, when the pole of the Earth was ninety degrees removed from the pole of the ecliptic. To those who can read aright, every lineament tells as plainly as the written word the history of that awful past, marking the march of time, recording the revolutions of the Sun in his orbit of 25,920 years, and relating with wonderful accuracy the climatic changes, in their lati-tudes, which took place with each revolution of the Sun and cor-responding motion of the Earth's pole of less than four degrees. All the greater myths of the dim past were formulated to express cosmic time, solar and polar motion, and the phenomena resulting therefrom. These monuments of antiquity prove that, the ancients knew a great deal more of the movements of heavenly bodies and of our planet than modern astronomers credit them with.

Madame Blavatsky, in her "Secret Doctrine," seriously states that all these monstrous forms are the types of actual, once living physical embodiments, and, with apparent sincerity, asserts that the Adepts teach such insane superstitions.

Such, however, is not the case, neither is there anything true, or even approaching the truth, in the cosmogony given in the work in question.

And, lastly, we have but one more aspect of the grand old Astro-Mythos to present to your notice. This aspect reveals the whole of the ancient classification of *work* and *labor,* and gives us a clear insight into the original designs, or pictorial representations, of the twelve signs and the twelve months of the year. It also clearly explains many things which are to-day attributed to superstitious paganism.

As each month possesses its own peculiar season, so are, or were, the various labors of the husbandman, and those of pastoral pursuits, altered and diverted. Each month, then, had a symbol which denoted the physical characteristics of climate and the temporal characteristics of work. As the Sun entered the sign, so the temple rites varied in honor of the labors performed, and the symbol thus became the object of outward veneration and worship. So we see that the twelve signs, and principally the four cardinal ones, became Deities, and the symbols sacred, but in reality, it was the same Sun to which homage was paid.

There is a large sphere of study in this direction, as, of course, each climate varied the symbol to suit its requirements. In Egypt there were three months when the land was overflowed with water; hence, they had only nine working months out of doors, and from this fact sprang the Nine Muses, while the Three Sirens represented the three months of inactivity in work, or three months of pleasure and festivity.

Mackey tells us that the great leviathan mentioned in the Book of Job was the river Nile.

In nearly all mythologies, we find that the gods assembled on some high mountain to take counsel. The Olympus of the Greeks and Mount Zion of the Hebrew Bible mean the same, the Pole-Star; and there, on the pictured planisphere, sits Cephus, the mighty Jove, with one foot on the Pole-Star and all the gods gathered below him. The Pole-Star is the symbol of the highest heaven.

With this we close, leaving the endless ramifications of this deeply interesting subject to the student's leisure and personal research, trusting the keys we have given in this chapter and their careful study may induce the reader and student of these pages to search out for himself the meaning concealed in all Astro-Mythologies.

CHAPTER VI

SYMBOLISM

At this point of our study it is necessary to make a halt; and, before proceeding further, to attempt to formulate and realize that, which, so far, we have been pursuing.

First, then, we have passed in review the Zodiac, and then the constellations. From this we mentally surveyed both Astro-Theology and Astro-Mythology; and now, it is our first duty to realize these in their real significance, and this consists in a clear comprehension of the Grand Law of Correspondences.

What is this law? It is the law of symbolism, and symbolism, rightly understood, is the one Divine language of Mother Nature, a language wherein all can read, a language that defies the united efforts of both time and space to obliterate it, for symbolism will be the language of Nature as long as spirit expresses itself to the Divine soul of man.

No matter where we turn nor where we look, there is spread out to our view a vast panorama of symbolic forms for us to read. In whatever form, angle, or color they present themselves, the true student of Nature can interpret and understand their symbolic language aright. It has been by the personification of Nature's symbols, that man has become ignorant of their language. There is no form, sound, nor color but what has its laws of expression; and only a perfect knowledge of symbolism will enable man to know the law, power, and meaning, lying behind such manifestations. The law of expression is exact, and as unalterable as Deity Himself. The physical senses cannot vibrate to these interior forces, and through them, comprehend their law. The physical senses vibrate to the spirit's expression, not to the powers, forces, and laws, which brought them into objective existence.

Countless numbers of mystics, if such they deserve to be called, among present-day students, speak and write very learnedly upon the "Law of Correspondence," and few, if any, of them really understand or know anything at all of that law. The intellect alone cannot solve the problems of this law. It cannot grasp the true, interior and spiritual meaning, except in just so far as intellect is capable of externalizing them. The inmost spiritual truths, that cannot be demonstrated to the outward senses, never have, nor never will, appeal to any one who has not the interior ability to comprehend them.

There was a time when men ruled by pure intellect, without its accompanying other half, intuition: they were looked upon as monstrosities. This state of purely intellectual development has been brought about by the positive, masculine principle, reason, absorbing its counterpart, the intuition, the feminine portion; and the result, by correspondence, is as fatal as upon the interior plane, where the positive, masculine soul denies the existence of his mate; thus setting upon his throne, only a portion of himself as his idol, and then, reasons himself into the belief that he is complete. Love has been cast out, ignored and forgotten until at last she departs, leaving a vacancy, that eternity cannot fill.

This is somewhat similar to their illusive Devachan, an ideal, a mere mystical sentiment to gush over, but a something they do not in reality comprehend. Therefore, we shall do our utmost to explain this universal law, and to point out wherein its first principles are manifest. Once these are mastered, the Golden Rule will explain all the rest: "As it is below, so it is above; as on the earth, so in the sky."

Here, then, is our first lesson on the subject of *reality,* which constitutes the Hermetic science of Correspondences.

First, realize that a line or an angle, for instance, is something more than its mere mathematical outline. It corresponds to some power, force, or principle within the great Anima-Mundi of the mysteries, that are trying to find expression, in their evolutionary journey, in forms. Let us illustrate our meaning. A point or dot is what? Well, externally it is the alpha of all mathematics. It is the first finite manifestation of the spiritual force. Within that dot lies concealed, in embryo, all the future possibilities of the manifesting principle.

This dot or point is a something to begin with, a form externalized, from which all future forms may spring forth, and they may be infinite, both in number and variety. First a primary, simple idea, from which all ideas and thoughts, intricate and complex, have their being.

A point extended is a straight line, scientifically expressed (whereas in real truth there is no such thing as a straight line); that is to say, it is a form increased or multiplied by itself, and therefore, is an extension in space that can be measured, and each extension means a new form, an additional symbol. It has taken on new aspects, new relations, hence contains the second principle of mathematics, so to say; but, besides being points, *they are symbols.* They are principles in Nature as clearly related to each other as the leaf and the stem of plant life.

Each monad, or point in the universe, is the beginning of something; equally so, it is also the termination of its own forces in that particular action, and will remain inert until it becomes acted upon by something else.

A point, then, is a primary, simple idea, a straight line. An angle is the same idea, rendered greater and more complex, and refers to the same forces upon a different plane, and the more we multiply the angles the more complex and far-reaching becomes the symbol and the more numerous and diverse become its planes of action. Here we will introduce an example. A trine represents three forces or angles, and, when united, form a trinity, hence harmony. Its apex (when above) is celestial, therefore represents the male forces of spirit.

A trine reversed also represents the same forces, with its apex in matter, hence it is negative. In these two complex ideas, clearly represented by these symbols, we have *all* matter and spirit; and yet they are but extensions of our point in space, rendered far-reaching and complex, by the position and the number of angles presented.

Let us turn the key once again, and we find that, both spirit and matter possess the same outline in their primal concept, except reversed (polarized).

Let us unite these two trines, and we have a still more potent form; a symbol almost infinitely complex. We have spirit and matter united, or, rather, three rays of force, positive, meeting three rays of force, negative, at a given point. Thus we have six points, also six sides, the ultimate of which is a cube. All are now equal. It is the first force of a crystallization (creation) of matter.

Once again let us turn the key, and we have our two conceptions in a metaphysical sense; the trine with its apex above is as the trine with its apex below, both the same in form, yet vibrating to very different planes, and a very different language is required to read and interpret their meaning aright. The spiritual, or the trine with its apex above, draws its influence from the celestial, and as it condenses and takes on form in the trine of matter, it transmits this same Divine force through its apex, which points below, to matter. The double trine is found upon every plane, obeying the Divine Law of Correspondences.

It is, in this sense, called "Solomon's Seal," because it is the grand hieroglyphic of the Hermetic law: "As it is above, so it is below; as on the Earth, so in the sky."

To continue this line of reasoning, or speculation, let us say, would lead us beyond the firm basis of human reason; it would escape the grasp of intellect, to which I am compelling this course of instruction to bend, but it would never take us beyond the real limits of the universe; yet, not to extend our investigations, we would ever remain in the lower trine, in the realms of effects, and lose sight entirely of the trine of spirit, from whence originated the force and potency in the form of matter.

Therefore it is, that the science of Symbolism has been evolved and formulated. The symbols, the manifestations, are ever present, and the study of effects will, to a developed soul, suggest the cause, the nature of the principle back of it, as well as the law which would produce such effects. Such is the science of symbolism; and it bounds and binds back into a religio-philosophical system, each class of symbols and each plane of manifestation; as securely as modern savants have defined the province of chemistry, magnetism, and mathematics; and, so far, these bounds are useful. But it is only a question of time and space, after all, because, when resolved back, or, let us say, evolved up into their abstract principles; chemistry, magnetism, and mathematics, are purely arbitrary terms to express special features of the same one eternal thing or science—which is *existence;* and it, in turn, is *consciousness;* not that external consciousness of existence, not that knowledge and love of living, but that interior, conscious knowledge, which tells us why and how we exist, by what force and power we are sustained and permitted to obey and carry out the law of mediumship, reception and transmission, attraction and repulsion, spiritual and material, that ultimately blend and become as one, the double trine, and, united with the Divine Ego of its being, becomes complete; seven, the perfected number of form.

The sum total, then, of all, and the value it may possess to the individual, is measured by his ability to perceive; for there is nothing external that is not in some sense mental, and there is nothing mental that is not in some sense spiritual. The sides of the triangle, physical, mental, and spiritual, and the apex where meet the mental and spiritual, forms the center of contact to higher trines in realms above.

Where mind is not, there are no symbols, no ideas, no manifestations. The spirit has not yet reached that point in its evolutionary journey where it can yet crystallize its projected force, power, or ideas, into forms; for everything that is, is the outcome of Divine thought, and expresses within itself the symbol of its being. This is the arcana of the Law of Correspondences.

Remember the above teaching, because upon its full comprehension rests the ability to read symbols aright. It will aid the soul to fully realize that, the vast universe is but the mental image of the Creator; that there is no such thing as manifested existence apart from mind; and consequently, the infinite worlds that float securely in space, blushing and scintillating with light of life and love of the Father, revealing to mortal minds some faint conception of the awful resources and recesses within Nature's star-making laboratory, are but the scintillating reflection of life, the reactions of mental phenomena. So, too, with the mental creative powers of the mind of man, for, not a vibration that proceeds from his every thought but what creates its correspondence in the creative realm of spirit. Hence, symbolism continues giving to the soul of man, throughout eternity, food for thought and contemplation.

All symbols, then, are objectified ideas, whether human or Divine; and as such possess a real meaning; and this meaning is altered, extended and rendered more complex with every additional thing or influence by which we find it surrounded, or with which, we find it correlated. For instance, $1.00 means one dollar; add six ciphers to the left 0000001., and it is still the same $1.00, and no more, because their position is previous, or before, the 1. But add the same number of ciphers to the right, $1,000000, and lo! we find a wondrous change of force, power, and consequence. We see all the mighty power of our million of money, and the possibilities and responsibilities with which, in these days, it becomes associated.

So it is with everything else in Nature. Man pays the penalty by increased responsibility, for every step in knowledge that he takes, as well as every dollar in gold he procures. Dollars, as well as talents, have to be accounted for, and their usefulness increased tenfold. The dollars must not be buried nor hoarded any more than our talents, but each, unfolded and doubled, so that we may be instrumental in helping our coworkers in their upward path, in the Cycle of Necessity. Knowledge is the basic foundation in reading Nature's language. Purity of thought, truth in motive, and unselfish benevolence, will lift the veil that now lies between the two trines, cause and effect, spirit and matter.

We have given the key and explained the alphabet of this wondrous law; therefore we close. Each must, by the same rules, work out the special links in the chain for him or herself. The angle from which each take their view determines the reading and interpretation of the symbols presented, whether that be from the apex, the sides or the base, for every symbol has its trinity in principles and form. Cause and effect are but the action and reaction; the result is the symbol which reveals the correspondence of both.

CHAPTER VII

What a weird yet strangely pleasing name the term Alchemy is. It is simple, yet so infilled and intermixed with the possible verities of exact science and the philosophical speculations on the infinite and the unknown, as to elude our mental grasp, as it were, by its own subtle essence, and defy the keenest analysis of our profoundest generalizers in science. And yet, in spite of this self-evident truth, how fascinating the sound of the word becomes to the mystic student's ear, and how pregnant with awful and mysterious possibilities it becomes, to the immortal powers embodied within the complex human organism termed man.

Words, if we but knew it, have the same innate, magnetic influence, and possess the same power of affinity and antipathy, that the human family possesses; as well as all organic and inorganic forms and substances; and how sad, to a developed soul, to witness the inharmony existing in our midst, caused by the misapplication of names.

Most human beings are very conscious of personal, or human magnetism, and its effects. But they stop right there, and do not dream of the subtle, silent influences emanating from a name, a word, and the power existing in words, when properly used. The human mind is so absorbed in Nature's manifestations, which are only the husks, that they fail to see the true, hidden meaning and realities, concealed beneath the material shell.

We will first notice the meaning of the words which constitute our subject, viz., Alchemy, then give a brief review of its physical correspondence, chemistry, and its true relation to its spiritual counterpart, Alchemy.

"Al" and "Chemy" are Arabic-Egyptian words which have much more in them than appears upon the surface, and possess a far different meaning from the one which the terms usually convey to the average mind. Terms, and the ideas we associate with them, vary according to the age in which we live. So with those, from which the word Alchemy is derived.

Let us penetrate beneath the mere verbal husk with which linguistic usage and convenience have clothed them, and which, in the course of ages, has become nothing but the dross of decomposed verbiage, and see if we can excavate the living germ, that has become buried within. If we can do so, we shall, at the commencement of our study, have attained unto a realization of the ancient meaning and real significance of the terms employed. And this will be no small gain, and will form no unimportant part of the equipment in our present research.

The Arabians, who derived the whole of their Occult arcana from the Egyptians, are the most likely to render us the most truthful and direct significance of the word, and so we find them. Thus, "Al," meaning "the," and Kimia," which means the hidden, or secret, *ergo* THE OCCULT, from which are derived our modern term Alchemy, more properly Al Kimia. This is very different from the popular conception to-day, which supposes that the word relates to the art of artificially making gold by some chemical process, and viewing it only as some sort of magical chemistry, forgetting that, the science of chemistry itself is also derived from the Kimia of Arabian mystics, and was considered as one and the same thing by every writer of the Middle Ages.

At this time, the physical man was not so dense and grasping for husks; hence the soul and spiritual part had greater control, and could impart the real, the alchemical side, of Nature to him; hence the Law of Correspondences was understood, and guided the educated in their considerations, researches, and conclusions.

Do you ask why, if they were so enlightened, they have veiled their knowledge from the world at large?

The power of mind over matter was as potent in those days as now, and the masses were as correspondingly corrupt as they are to-day. Therefore, to put this knowledge into the hands of the multitude would have been generally disastrous. So they wrote it in mystical language, knowing that all educated students in Nature's laws, at that time, would understand; yet they little dreamed how much their language would be misunderstood in the centuries to follow, by those who look to their ancient ancestry for aid on subjects that have become at the present day so lost in mystery.

Having ascertained, beyond question, that Alchemy was, and consequently is, the secret science of Occultism—not the philosophy, mind you, but the science; let us proceed, for, we shall find that these two aspects may often differ, or appear to differ, widely from each other, though they can never do so in reality, for the latter produces and establishes the facts, while the former occupies itself in their tabulation and deductions. The science constitutes the foundation, and the philosophy, the metaphysical speculations, which rest thereon. If these important distinctions are borne in mind, all the apparent confusion, contradiction, and other intellectual debris, will either disappear or resolve themselves into their own proper groups, so that we may easily classify them.

It is at this very point, that, so many students go astray amid the labyrinths of science and philosophy. They, unconsciously, so mix and intermingle the two terms, that nine-tenths of the students present only one side of the question—philosophy, which soon runs into theory, if not supported by the science, which they have lost in their volumes of philosophy.

You may say, one subject at a time. Yes, this may be true, if its twin brother is not absorbed and forgotten.

In this chapter, we shall deal especially with organic Alchemy.

Organic Alchemy deals exclusively with living, organic things, and in this connection differs from the Alchemy of inorganic matter. These two aspects may, in this one respect, be compared to organic and inorganic chemistry, to which originally they belonged; as astrology did to astronomy. Alchemy and astrology—twin sisters—were the parents of the modern offspring, known in chemistry and astronomy as exact science. These latter, however, deal with shadows and phenomenal illusions, while the former concern the living realities, which produce them. Therefore, there can be "no new thing under the sun," saith Solomon.

First, let us deal with the most lovely form of our art, that which pertains to the floral and vegetable kingdoms. Every flower or blade of grass, every tree of the forest and stagnant weed of the swamp, is the outcome of, and ever surrounded by, its corresponding degree of spiritual life. There is not a single atom but what is the external expression of some separate, living force, within the spaces of Æth, acting in unison with the dominant power corresponding with the type of life.

If science could only behold this wonderful laboratory within the vital storehouse of Nature, she would no longer vainly seek for *the origin of life*, nor wonder, what may have become of the missing link in scientific evolution, because, she would quickly realize that, biogenesis is the one grand truth of both animate and inanimate Nature, the central, living source of which is God. Science would also, further realize that, this biune life is ever in motion throughout the manifested universe; circulating around the focii of creative activities, which we term suns, stars, and planets, awaiting the conditions which are ever present for material incarnation; and under all possible combinations of circumstances and conditions, conceivable and inconceivable, adapting itself to continuous phenomenal expression. Links, so called, in this mighty chain of evolution, may appear to be missing here and there, and, for that matter, whole types may seem to be wanting, but, this is only because of our imperfect perception, and, in any case, can make no real difference with the facts, because, if such be a reality, if there be what *we* may term *missing links* in the scheme of evolution, it only shows that spirit, although associated with, is ever independent of matter.

But matter—what is to become of it? Is it independent of spirit? The kindness of the Divine spirit heeds not the unconscious mind of matter and its boasted independence, and works silently on, and at last, accomplishes its mission—the evolution of matter, the uplifting of the soul of man, as well as the universe. The blindness of man is dense, and the saddest part to admit is that, they will so stubbornly remain so.

If, for one instant, the penetrating eye of the soul could shine forth through the physical orbs of vision, and imprint the scenes, beheld behind the veil, upon the tablets of the brain of the physical organism, a fire would be kindled that, could never be quenched by the fascinating allurements of the material, perishable things, of matter.

That development of the real atom of biune life can, and does, go forward, irrespective of the gradation of physical types, needs no convincing proof, other than visible Nature.

Man is not the outcome of physical evolution, and produced by a series of blind laws, that lead him upward from protozoa to man, as a child climbs up stairs, advancing regularly, *one step as a time.* This latter conception, we know, is the theory of exact science, but not of Alchemy, not of the science of Occultism. Man, according to Wallace, Darwin, Huxley, and Tyndall, is what progressive stages of physical evolution have made him. But the very reverse is true. The fauna

and flora of past geological periods are what the human soul has
produced, by virtue of its gradual advancement to higher states and
conditions of life, so that, so far from man being the outcome of the
planet's development, such material progress is the outgrowth of man's
advancement, proving again that, matter is not independent of spirit,
neither can spirit be independent of matter for its expressions. They
so interblend that, the dividing line cannot be detected by the untrained eye of the exact scientist. But, that time is not far distant,
when the scientists will prepare and evolve their interior being to
take up the spiritual thread, exactly where the visible thread ends,
and carry forth the work, as far as the mortal mind of man can penetrate, while embodied in the physical form.

God hasten this day is my prayer, for then man will become
more spiritual and aspiring for advancement and knowledge, thus,
setting up vibrations that will create higher and loftier conditions for
the physical man. Aye! then they will know that, even the birth of
the world itself, owes its primal genesis to the desire of the human
atom for earthly embodiment.

Here is where exact science, or the counterpart of Alchemy, becomes both profitable and helpful. Says Paracelsus: "The true use of
chemistry is not to make gold, but to prepare medicines." He admits
four elements—the *star,* the *root,* the *element* and the *sperm.* These
elements were composed of the three principles, *sideric salt, sulphur,*
and *mercury.* Mercury, or spirit, sulphur, or oil, and salt, and the
passive principles, water and earth. Herein we see the harmony of the
two words, Alchemy and Chemistry. One is but the continuation of
the other, and they blend so into each other that, they are not complete, apart.

The chemist, in his analysis of the various component parts of
any form of matter, knows also the proportional combinations; and
thus, by the Law of Correspondence, could, by the same use of the
spiritual laws of Alchemy, analyze and combine the same elements
from the atmosphere, to produce the corresponding expression of
crystallized form. By the same laws, are affinities and antipathies
discovered and applied, in every department of Nature's wonderful
laboratory.

Chemistry is the physical expression of Alchemy, and any true
knowledge of chemistry is:—not the knowing of the names of the ex-

tracts and essences, and the plants themselves, and that certain combinations produce certain results, obtained from blind experiments, yet, prompted by the Divine spirit within; but, knowledge born from knowing the why and wherefore of such effects. What is called the oil of olives is not a single, simple substance, but it is more or less combined with other essential elements, and will fuse and coalesce with other oils and essences of similar nature. The true chemist will not confine his researches for knowledge to the mere examination, analysis, and experiments, in organic life; but will inform himself equally, in physical astrology; and learn the nature, attributes, and manifested influences of the planets, that constitute our universe; and, under which, every form of organic matter is subject, and especially, controlled by. Then, by learning the influence of the planets upon the human family; and that special planetary vibration that influences the individual; he can intelligently and unerringly administer medicines to remove disease in man.

A familiarity with the mere chemical relations of the planet to man, makes still more apparent, the mutual affinity of both to the soil, from which they appear to spring, and to which, they ultimately return; so much so that, we have become conscious, that, the food we eat is valuable or otherwise as a life sustainer, in proportion to the amount of life it contains. We are so complex in our organization that, we require a great variety of the different elements to sustain all the active functions and powers within us. Man, being a microcosm, or a miniature universe, must sustain that universe, by taking into the system the various elements, which combine to make up the Infinite Universe of God. Animal flesh is necessary to certain organized forms, both animal and man. When I say necessary, I do not mean an acquired taste and habit of consuming just so much flesh a day; but a constitution, which would not be complete in its requirements, without animal flesh. I am thankful such do not constitute the masses.

Science would say, you only require certain combinations of oxygen, hydrogen, nitrogen, and carbon, to sustain all the activities of the physical body. Apparently, this is true. Upon the surface it is, but in reality it is not; because if it were really true there could be no famines. Science could make bread out of stones, as was suggested at the temptation of Christ in the wilderness. And yet, no one knows better than the academies of Science, themselves, that their

learned professors would quickly starve to death, if they were compelled to produce their food from the chemical properties of the rocks.
They can make a grain of wheat chemically perfect, but they cannot
make the invisible germ by which it will grow, become fruitful, and
reproduce itself. They can reproduce from the stones in the street the
same chemical equivalents that go to compose gluten, albumen, and
starch—the trinity which must always be present to sustain life; but
they cannot, by any known process, make such chemical equivalents
of these substances, do the same thing. Now, if not, why not? Science
cannot answer this. A very mysterious shake of the head and profound silence is the only answer. Ask Science *how the plant grows*,
what causes the atoms of matter to build up root, stem, leaf, bud and
flower, true to the parent species from which the germinal atom came.
What is there behind the plant that stamps it with such striking individuality? And why, from the same soil, the deadly aconite and
nutritious vegetable can grow, each producing qualities in harmony
with its own nature, so widely different in their effects upon the human
organism, *yet, so completely identical as regards the source from which
they appear to spring.* There must be a something to account for this,
and this something, ancient Alchemy alone can scientifically reveal and
expound; and, this knowledge lies just beyond that line which calls a
halt to material scientists, and says: "You can go no farther; this is
beyond your purview. The end of the material thread has been
reached, and unless you can connect it with the thread of the next
plane, your researches must stop."

Before entering upon and answering these vital questions, we
must digress a little, and make ourselves perfectly familiar with the
ideas and revelations of advanced physical science upon the subject, and for this purpose no more trustworthy guide can be consulted
than the new edition of "The Chemistry of Common Life," by the
late James F. W. Johnson, M. A., England, and revised by Arthur
Herbert Church, M. A. In chapter IV on page 56 of this work, upon
the anatomy of plant life, we read:

"How interesting it is to reflect on the minuteness of the organs
by which the largest plants are fed and sustained. Microscopic aper-
tures in the leaf suck in gaseous food from the air; the surfaces of
microscopic hairs suck a liquid food from the soil. We are accustomed
to admire, with natural and just astonishment, how huge, rocky reefs,

hundreds of miles in length, can be built up by the conjoined labors of myriads of minute zoophytes, laboring together on the surface of a coral rock; but it is not less wonderful that, by the ceaseless working of similar microscopic agencies in leaf and root, the substance of vast forests should be built up and made to grow before our eyes. It is more wonderful, in fact; for whereas, in the one case, the chief result is that, dead matter extracted from the sea is transformed into a dead rock; in the other, the lifeless matter of the earth and air are converted by these minute plant-builders into living forms, lifting their heads aloft to the sky, waving with every wind that blows, and beautifying whole continents with the varying verdure of their ever-changing leaves."

Further on in the same chapter, on pages 62-3, the same eloquent writer continues:

"But the special chemical changes that go on within the plant, could we follow them, would appear not less wonderful than the rapid production of entire microscopic vegetables from the raw food contained in the juice of the grape. It is as yet altogether incomprehensible, even to the most refined physiological chemistry, how, from the same food taken in from the air, and from generally similar food drawn up from the soil, different plants, and different parts of plants, should be able to extract or produce substances so very different from each other in composition and in all of their properties. From the seed-vessels of one (the poppy) we collect a juice which dries up into our commercial opium; from the bark of another (cinchona) we extract the quinine with which we assuage the raging fever; from the leaves of others, like those of hemlock and tobacco, we distil deadly poisons, often of rare value for their medicinal uses. The flowers and leaves of some yield volatile oils, which we delight in for their odors and their aromatic qualities; the seeds of others give fixed oils, which are prized for the table or use in the arts * * * These, and a thousand other similar facts, tell us how wonderfully varied are the changes which the same original forms of matter undergo in the interior of living plants. Indeed, whether we regard the vegetable as a whole, or examine its minutest part, we find equal evidence of the same diversity of changes and of the same production, in comparatively minute quantities, of very different, yet often characteristic forms of matter."

From the whole of the foregoing, we observe the exact position
to be the one we have previously stated. If such wondrous things
can be revealed to us through the physical science of chemistry, what
think you must be hidden from our physical sight and knowledge by
the veil which hangs between matter and spirit? Think you not, it is
worth the effort to penetrate beyond that point where the atom dis-
appears from the view of the scientist?

If plants produce such wonderful phenomena in their life and
influence, what must the Divine organism of man have concealed
within his microscopic universe, to study and comprehend? Plant life
is merely the alphabet of the complex, intricate, and multitudinous
processes, going on in the human body.

And, as the mechanical microscope of physical science cannot
reveal the why and the wherefore, let us, for a brief moment, disclose
some of the wonders that declare their existence, when subjected to
the pentrating alchemical lens, of the inward spirit. The first thing
that intrudes itself upon our notice, by virtue of its primary importance, is the grand fact of biogenesis—life emanating from life. We
perceive every external form to be the physical symbol of a corresponding degree of spiritual life; that each complete plant represents
a complete cycle, state, or degree of interior existence; that it is made
up and consists of countless millions of separate atoms of life; that
these atoms of spiritual activity are the real instigators of the life and
motion of corresponding material atoms; that they ever obey the
Divine impluse of co-operative unity, in their chemical, as well as
their spiritual affinity. Consequently, everything in the form of material substance must be, and is, but the means for the phenomenal
expression of incarnating spirit; the organism of man, a tree, a plant,
or an animal, being no exception to this Divine, omnipresent law of
creative life.

To the true Alchemist there can be no mystery surrounding the
wonderful phenomena mentioned in the work we have quoted, in
plants extracting from the same rocks, soil, and air, qualities so mani-
festly different—deadly poisons, healing balsams, and pleasant aromas,
or the reverse, from the same identical plant foods. Nothing is more
wonderful or mysterious, than, the same alchemical processes, which,
are hourly being enacted within our own bodies. From the same
breath of air and the same crust of bread do we concoct the blood,

the bile, the gastric juice, and various other secretions; and distil the finer nervous fluids, that go to build up and sustain the whole of our mental and dynamic machinery. It is the same ancient story of the atoms; each part and each function endowing the same inorganic chemicals with their own spiritual, magnetic, and physical life-qualities, by what appears, to the uninitiated observer, a miraculous transmutation of matter, but which is, in reality, the evolution of organic form from inorganic materials, in obedience to the Divine law of spiritual progression. Who could stop with exact science? For, when we come to consider the apparent mysteries of life and growth by the aid of this alchemical light, the shadows flee, and all the illusions of Nature's phenomenal kaleidoscope vanish before the revelation of the underlying spiritual realities. We know that the plant, being the physical expression upon the material plane of a more interior life, endows its outward atoms with their peculiar qualities. *These qualities are not drawn directly from the soil;* the soil only becoming the medium for their complete or incomplete expression, as the case may be; i.e., supplying the necessary inorganic atoms. Hence, the deadly qualities of aconite, and the generous life-sustaining qualities of the nutritious vegetable, *being spiritual life endowments,* conveyed to the material substance, abstracted from the soil and withdrawn from the atmosphere, are no mystery; their effect upon the human organism being exactly that, which is produced by their spiritual affinity or antipathy, as the case may be. And this also shows and explains, why purely inorganic chemical atoms, though they be exactly the same as the organic substances, from a strictly scientific standpoint, *yet fail to support life,* because such chemical equivalents lack the organic spirituality of the interior life, which alone, gives them the power and function to support the same. They fail to fulfill the requirements of the alchemical law of life for the support of life—in other words, biogenesis.

And, too, this inorganic life may be parted from the plant or vegetable, if it be too long severed from the medium which transmits the spiritual life, from the inorganic world to that of organic matter. Vegetables, fresh from the ground, or parent stem, retain this life if at once prepared for food, if not overcooked, which is so often ignorantly done. This is the secret of sustenance from foods. Nature's perfected fruits and vegetables are overflowing with the life-giving essences, and, if eaten direct from the tree or parent stem, that life is not lost, but transmitted to our organisms, and replenishes the wasting system with a living life. Much less of such food is required to completely satisfy and nourish the body than if the life had partly departed or been destroyed.

Briefly stated, then, everything within organic Nature is the expressional symbolic manifestation of spirit; every form being a congregation of innumerable atoms of life, revealing their presence in material states; each organic form, or, rather, organism, evolving under the central control of some dominating Deific atom or soul, which, by virtue of past incarnations and labors in its cycle of evolution, from the mineral up to man, has achieved the royal prerogative to rule within its own state. Man being the highest representative form—the grand finale in the earthly drama—sums up and contains within himself everything below, and *the germs of everything beyond, this state.* He is truly a microcosm, and represents in miniature the grand Cosmic Man of the Heavens. Every living force beneath him corresponds to some state, part, or function, which he has graduated through and conquered, and which, in him, has now become embodied, as a part of his universal kingdom. Consequently, all things are directly related to him, in the grand universal unity of spiritual life.

This cannot be realized and comprehended by the physical man, nor conveyed to his outer senses by the physical sciences. He must bring into active use the inner man, the real being, which inhabits and controls the outer organism, and through its instrumentality, understand the interior source and workings behind the phenomena of manifested being. So we see that, exact science cannot take us far, yet, it is a mighty factor, in the evolution of the microcosm Man, and in consciously relating him to the Infinite Macrocosm—God, Spirit, All.

CHAPTER VIII

Paracelsus, the most celebrated of the alchemists of the Middle Ages, thus mystically speaks of his art:

"If I have manna in my constitution, I can attract manna from heaven. Melissa is not only in the garden, but also in the air and in heaven. Saturn is not only in the sky, but also deep in the ocean and Earth. What is Venus but the artemisia that grows in your garden, and what is iron but the planet Mars? That is to say, Venus and Artemisia are both products of the same essence, while Mars and iron are manifestations of the same cause. What is the human body but a constellation of the same powers that formed the stars in the sky? He who knows Mars knows the qualities of iron, and he who knows what iron is knows the attributes of Mars. What would become of your heart if there were no Sun in the Universe? What would be the use of your 'Vasa Spermatica'° if there were no Venus? To grasp the invisible elements, to attract them by their material correspondences, to control, purify, and transmute, them by the ever-moving powers of the living spirit—this is true Alchemy."

Thus, in a very few simple words, we find this master of the art revealing the whole arcana of that mysterious science, which has for its chief object and goal, the discovery of the "philosopher's stone," which confers upon its fortunate possessor the blessings of immortal youth. Therefore, we cannot possibly do better in the commencement of our present study than, to minutely examine each particular sentence and endeavor to discover his true meaning, which, like all mystical writing, is so apparent, yet cunningly concealed, as to excite the student's admiration.

"If I have manna in my constitution, I can attract manna from Heaven." The manna here spoken of does not specify any particular thing, but is of universal application, and is simply used as an unknown quantity, like x, y, z in mathematics. But, ever since the days of Paracelsus, half-initiated mystics and bookworm Occultists, have endeavored to discover what this manna really was. Some, the more

------

°Astral germs of subjective life forms:—it is the latent, "to be".

spiritual, were of the opinion that, it was spiritual power, or purity of spirit; others imagined it to mean special magnetic qualifications, similar in nature to the so-called gifts of modern spiritualistic media. The concealment of the truth is unique, and consists in its very simplicity; and, when correctly expounded, should read: "I am the microcosm, and all the visible and invisible universe dwells within me, so that whatsoever power I have in my constitution, I can attract its correspondence from Heaven." Paracelsus must have smiled to himself when he wrote "*If I have manna,*" etc., because his whole writings strive to prove man the miniature of Deity. Further along, he explains himself by pointing out the real Law of Correspondence, thus: "Melissa is not only in the garden, but also in the air, and in Heaven. Saturn is not only in the sky, but also deep in the ocean, and Earth." The illustrations are beautiful. The life of the plant, the "anima floralis," pervades the atmosphere and the interior states of spiritual life, where it becomes in the highest degree beautiful, and beneficial to the soul. A reference upon this point to "The Light of Egypt" Vol., I, may not be considered out of place. Upon page 74 it is written: "The flower that blooms in beauty, breathing forth to the air its fragrance, which is at once grateful to the senses and stimulating to the nerves, is a perfect specimen of Nature's faultless mediumship. The flower is a medium for the transmission to the human body of those finer essences, and of *their spiritual portion to the soul;* for the aroma of the flower is spiritualized to such a degree as to act upon the life currents of the system, imparting to the spiritual body a nutriment of the finest quality."

Thus, here is where the knowledge of the alchemical attributes of plants, as applicable to man, can be most beneficially utilized. Plants and flowers, whose attributes and aromas harmonize with the complex organism of man, should be selected for the house and garden, for, they are mediums to transmit the finer essences and aromas to the spiritual constitution of man; the plant to the physical, and the aromas and essences of the flowers to the soul.

Antipathies in plants and flowers would bring a similar evil influence, as the discords of the antagonistic human magnetism. It would not be so apparent, but more subtle, yet nevertheless effective in result.

Our attention is next drawn to the planet Saturn, which, we are informed, is not only shining in his starry sphere of the heavens, but is also buried in the ocean depths and embodied in the stratas of the earth. It is almost needless to add that, our author refers to those substances naturally Saturnine in their quality of life and expression, such as lead, clay, and coal, among the minerals, and various deadly plants among the flora, the chief of which is the aconite or *monkshood*, so significant of Saturn and the isolated, monkish hermit. After some repetition, in order to impress the truth of correspondences, our author exclaims: "What is the human body but a constellation of the same powers that formed the stars in the sky?" Truly, what else? for, "he who knows Mars knows the qualities of iron, and he who knows what iron is knows the attributes of Mars." Could anything be plainer? We think not.

From the foregoing, which a long experience and much critical investigation and research have demonstrated as true, we cannot avoid the conclusion that Alchemy, equally as well as every other science, religion, or system of philosophy formulated by man, resolves itself, ultimately, in all its final conclusions, into the one universal parent of all wisdom.

ASTROLOGY, the Science of the Stars, in unison with the Science of the Soul, was, and still is, the one sublime center of real learning. It constituted the sacred fountain of living waters, from whose placid depths there rayed forth the Divine revelations of man, his whence, where, and whither; and under the careful conservation of a long line of gifted seers, it shone forth to the sons of men, as the sacred Hermetic light in the Astro-Masonic wisdom of Egypt's ancient priesthood.

It is not lost to us to-day. The same book lies open before us that faced our ancient forefathers. It is standing out clear and distinct, waiting to be read by the sons of men. We can learn its language, and from its pages, we ourselves can read our relation to God and our fellowman. Shall we not heed the whispering intuitions of the soul and place ourselves in conscious rapport with the whole?

This sublime Book of Wisdom was written by God Himself, to convey to His children the knowledge of His powers, attributes, and relation to all creative life. We cannot see that Divine Spirit which we call God. No; but as long as the finite form exists as such, we will have the spirit's manifestations to learn from. Never will the Book of God be closed to the searching eye of the soul. There will always be presented to his vision lessons to study, and practical experiments to perform, to lead the soul into deeper mysteries. Until man fathoms his own universe, he cannot understand God. "Know thyself" is as applicable to-day as when the famous, immortal and mystic utterance was inscribed on the porch of the temple at Delphi.

Before this wonderful, divinely elaborated, but complex system can be fully realized, it is necessary that the student should comprehend, very distinctly, the two states of existence, the internal and the external, and become familiar with the laws of correspondences. And it seems strange that of all Sciences, that of medicine should have so completely failed to grasp this living truth, since every atom of medicine administered, invariably acts upon this alchemical principle. When the human organism has become discordant in some of its parts, it is because the interstellar vibrations have aroused various states within the human kingdom into a condition of rebellion against the supreme will. Man's ignorance favors such seditious movements, and his general habits and code of morals stimulate them to undue activity. The final result is *disease*—disorganization of the parts and functions, and those medicines corresponding *to the same functional degree of life within the grand man,* cure the disorder, when administered properly and *in time,* whereas, if given to the perfectly healthy organism, *the atoms produce similar symptoms to the diseases they alleviate,* because it is their mission to either subdue or be subdued, and when disease prevails the medicinal atoms, acting in unison with the natural parts and functions they affect, conquer or subdue the inharmony, and vice versa, as before stated. In all cases of disease and medicine, it is a simple question of *a war between the atoms,* and, therefore, the most potential forces within Nature are always at the command of the true Alchemist, because he knows how and when to select his fighting forces, and when to set them in motion, for the best results.

Hahnemann, the founder of the Homeopathic system, has approached *the nearest* to this alchemical truth, and as a consequence, we find it is in actual practice, the most natural, scientific, and successful system of medicine, yet given to the world; based, as it is, upon the well-known law of affinites, "*Similia similibus curantur,*" "like cures like," being a very ancient axiom in the astrological practice of physic.

Bulwer Lytton, who had become thoroughly convinced of the great value and importance of uniting ancient Alchemy with modern medicine, makes the hero of his immortal story declare: "All that we propose to do is this: To find out the secrets of the human frame, to know why the parts ossify and the blood stagnates, and to apply continual preventives to the effects of time. *This is not magic; it is the art of medicine, rightly understood."*

It is a fact that, the molecules of the body are all changed within twelve months; that every cell in the human organism is born and grows to maturity within that space of time. Nature is absolutely impartial. She draws from the atmosphere that she may reproduce a fac-simile of everything she finds upon the surface of the body. So, if there be a sore, or festering ulcer, the atoms which are thrown off attract similar atoms, so as to reproduce the ulcer or sore, and thus prevent the disease from getting well of itself until it has worn itself out.

Further, every vein and canal throughout the entire body, from youth to maturity, is being coated with carbonate of lime, or lime in some form. The coating of the walls of the veins in such a manner, prevents the free circulation of the living matter; then, the real vitality of the food which we eat, is simply passed off through the pores, or through the bowels, or through the system, because it is unable to penetrate through the lime.

If that prevention which produces old age can be attained, then physical youth will continue.

The first step to take is to dissolve the lime in the body. Drink nothing but distilled water, in either tea, coffee, or any other form, and drink freely of the sweet juices of the grape and apple.

The food that we eat contains lime in a living form, and it is the living lime we need to build up the living bones, for the lime and the magnesia that we take in the water is crystallized dead mineral, possessing no responsibility of life, and the lime in our food is quite sufficient for all purposes. For everything we take in excess, Nature makes us pay the penalty.

The first principle of long living is to keep all channels of the body perfect and free from coatings of lime.

The second is that of youthful ideals of the mind. The soul never grows old.

The third principle is dynamic breathing, which is storing up the oxygen in sufficient quantities, to supply the tissues with sufficient fuel, for combustion.

These three principles, acting in unison, contain the true basis of physical life and a means of long living. Old age is simply the petrifaction of the body through lime, and the incorporating of erroneous thoughts into the organism.

It is the true Alchemy of human existence, and the preventives, in each and every case must contain the spiritual correspondence to the cause they seek to remedy; and, though the followers of Hahnemann base the whole of their procedure of treatment upon their master's fundamental law of "Similia similibus curantur," yet, there may be a few rare cases wherein, this undeviating method would not apply with the required effect. In such a case, the Alchemist would resort to the well-known law of opposites, and base his treatment upon the dogma of "Contraria contrariis curantur," so long the pet theory of the Allopathic school. They work upon the hypothesis that, like attracts like, and, if disease exist, those elements must be administered to set up the vibrations that will produce the polar opposite. If the body was racked with pain, those medicines would not be given that would create or increase similar conditions, but, their antipathy would be introduced into the system or applied locally to extinguish the foe.

So long as mankind remain within the semicrystallized state of soul development, so as to require the aid of external forces to support the human throne within its earthly temple, mercenary troops will exist to supply these supposed supports.

Unquestionably, the astrological law is the true system of medicine, which treats disease by sympathy or by antipathy, according to the nature of the case, and the efficacy of the remedies at hand. This method is the only natural one, and has been thoroughly demonstrated by the numerous "provings of drugs" under Hahnemann's law.

Happily, the time is not far distant when, the incarnated spirit will be able to use its own slumbering forces, and subdue all suffering and symptoms of disease in their very first inception, by virtue of its purer life and the dynamic potencies of its own interior, spiritual thought. Already, mental therapeutics is taking an advanced position among liberal, progressive minds, and nothing demonstrates so clearly and forcibly the grand, alchemical law of life-growth and decay, as the imponderable, invisible forces, which, constitute the materia medica, or remedial agents, of mental, magnetic, and spiritual healing.

Perhaps the most recondite subject connected with the healing art divine is, the modus operandi of medicinal action, upon the human body. A subject so simple and self-evident to the Alchemist, remains a profound mystery to the educated physician of the medical college; so much so that, we are tempted to ask of them: "Can you explain the modus operandi of drugs?" Dr. William Sharp, one of the most advanced physicians of the Homeopathic school, in one of his well-known "Essays on Medicine," says: "In respect to the manner of action of drugs we are in total darkness, and we are so blind that the darkness is not felt. *Knowledge of this kind cannot be attained;* it is labor lost and *time wasted* to go in search of it. True, hypotheses may be easily conceived; so may straws be gathered from the surface of the stream. But what are either of them worth? There is this difference between them—straws may amuse children, and hypotheses are sure to mislead physicians."

It is when the Occult Initiate observes to what helpless conditions the practice of medicine has fallen, that, he would, if he could with any possiblity of success, implore the angelic guardian of the human race to open the spiritual sight of men, that they might see, as he sees, the Divine relationship, and spiritual correspondence, of everything in the wide universe to man.

Nature's laws move slowly and imperceptibly, yet surely and exact, and the time will certainly come when man will be forced into consciousness of these laws, whether he will or no. Nature is no respecter of persons, and those who will not move and progress, in harmony with her laws of advancement, must, of necessity, pass out with the old.

Alchemy, as it relates to the healing art, is the most noble in its object and beneficial in its effects, of all the many subdivisions of the sciences, because, it alleviates the pains and morbid afflictions of suffering humanity. We have given quite sufficient of its astrological aspect in the second part of "The Light of Egypt," Vol. I, wherein the four ancient elements are translated into their chemical correspondences of oxygen, hydrogen, nitrogen and carbon, which still constitute the four primary elements of the most advanced chemistry to-day. They enter more or less into every organic form and substance, which is known, in various combinations and proportions. The human organism is principally composed of them; so, likewise, is the food that supports physical life, and the air we breathe is but modifications of the same atoms.

As man's constitution embraces a microscopic atom of all the essences and elements, corresponding to the whole; so does the air; and much, that we depend upon our food to supply, can be extracted from the atmosphere by breathing. Every breath we breathe is new life, or death.

Herein is the secret of success or failure, in certain localities, and under certain conditions. If we have iron within us, could we extract or attract iron from Saturn's district? Or, if the element within us could attract gold, could we obtain it from the coal fields?

Therefore, it is only natural that the medical remedies we employ to restore the organism, when afflicted with disease, should group themselves into similar correspondences, and so, in a general sense, we find them; for we note that the brain, the circulation, the lungs, and the stomach, are the four chief citadels of the body; the heart, of course, representing the center of circulation. And this also explains, further, if that were necessary, why the principal remedies of the homeopathic system are so speedy and direct in their action. The four principal drugs, which stand as representatives of their class, are aconite, belladonna, phosphorus, and pulsatilla. These represent the quadrant, for light is not more nicely adjusted to the eye, nor sound to the ear, than aconite to the circulation, belladonna to the brain, phosphorus to the lungs, and pulsatilla to the stomach; while ramifying in the seven directions indicated by the seven primary planets, we find stimulants, tonics, narcotics, nervines, alteratives, cathartics and diuretics, as the natural material correspondences thereof.

That we assign phosphorus to the lungs may appear startling to the orthodox student, especially when, he calls to mind the fact that phosphorus has long been recognized in medical science as a brain food and medicine. Anticipating such mental questions, we reply that in medicine, from the alchemical view, we are occupying a wholly different standpoint; i.e., the power of controlling the functional action of the body, in this view of the case, and the fact that, the lungs and the brain are in the most perfect affinity, there will remain no mystery upon the subject.

The Alchemy of stones and gems attracts our next attention. Affinites and antipathies to the human constitution, are to be found in these crystallized representatives of the subtle, invisible influences emanating from our planetary system. They are the mediums for the transmission of corresponding attributes and influences of existing powers and potencies, and if carried or worn upon the person, they will bring the person in direct rapport with the invisible forces within the universal system.

Here again Hahnemann's scientific philosophy would prove effectual, that "Similia similibus curantur." Would the fiery influence of a topaz attract much from the realms of a chrysolite? Or, the crystallized, airy forces of a sapphire be a suitable medium for the earthly forces of a jasper?

Gems and stones are dead or living realities. They live, slumber and die, and have their potent existence as do the organic forms of matter. They are, usually, imbued with the vivifying spark of Divinity, and shine forth and exert their influence through the magical powers attracted to them from the forces of Nature. A real, living entity abides within them that can be seen by the clairvoyant vision, and to the trained student in Occult lore, this entity can be made to become an obedient servant, giving warning of the approach of danger, impressions of men and things, and warding off discordant influences surrounding us; or that, which we may contact from the magnetic and personal environments in our relations in the social world; or that which may be projected to us from the invisible realms of life.

Think you the pryamids would be intact to-day, if the stones from which they were built had been promiscuously selected? They were chosen by Adepts in the knowledge of the Laws of Correspondence and antipathy and affinity. The sphinx also stand as monuments to the heights of wisdom that man can attain.

Metals also can be followed out on the same lines as the gems and stones.

Much as we would like to continue, we are compelled to bring this discourse to a close, even though in doing so we must of necessity omit much of vital interest to the student. We will, therefore, only add that the seven basic metals stand as the crystallized representatives of their respective groups: Gold for the Sun, Silver for the Moon, Tin for Jupiter, Copper for Venus, Quicksilver for Mercury, Lead for Saturn and Iron for Mars. Each finds its own sphere of action within the temporary abiding place of the human soul on earth—the physical body. So, likewise, the twelve constallations and their corresponding talismanic gems, representing in their glittering array the anatomical Zodiac of the human frame, and typifying the spiritual quality of the atoms, there congregated, in every degree of life. These, and a thousand other mysteries, had we the time, might be unfolded to the student's view with considerable advantage, but we are compelled to refrain. The philosopher's stone is near at hand. Seek it not in remote spheres or distant parts of the earth, for it is ever around you and within, and becomes the golden key of true wisdom, which prepares the soul for its higher life and brighter destiny. It is the still, small voice of the awakened soul, that purges the conscience from suffering, and the spiritual body from earthy dross. It is that, which treasures not the corrupting, delusive wealth of Earth, nor the transient powers of mammon, but garners the fruits which spring from the pure life, and treasures the jewels of heaven. Vainly will you seek for this stone of the wise philosopher amid the turmoils, sufferings, and selfishness of life, unless you accept your mission upon earth as a duty, delegated to the soul, from Heaven. Eschew the evil thereof, and hold fast that which is good. To do this, means to expand with the inward truth and become one of the "pure in heart," in which blessed state, the magical white stone, conveying *a new name,* reveals the living angel within, to the outward man. Then, and then alone, doth he know the Adonai.

Such are the Divine, spiritual principles upon which the higher Alchemy of life is based. They seek only to establish a Divine, conscious at-one-ment between the angel, the man, and the universe, and to this end, we conclude with the words of the immortal Paracelsus:

"To grasp these invisible elements, to attract them by their material correspondences, to control, purify, and transmute them by the ever-moving powers of the living spirit, *this is true Alchemy.*"

CHAPTER IX

TALISMANS

Words are the symbols of ideas, and bear the same correspondence to the physical brain as matter does to spirit, a medium of expression, and are subject to continual change in their application and meaning, in exact proportion to the changing mental and moral condition of the people. As the planet, as well as man, is continually progressing, so must there be a higher and nobler conception of ideas. Hence, words or expressions must change, to convey the progressive spirit, that is constantly taking place. Therefore, it is always interesting, as well as valuable, for the Occult student to go to the root of each word connected with his philosophy, in order to learn the real sense in which the word was used by the ancients, from whom his mystic lore has descended. The true meaning, as well as the words themselves, have become as mystical as the lore itself. Hence, each student must commence as a beginner in any foreign language, which he does not at present understand. In following this method of procedure he will, at least, escape the dense and interminable confusion of modern opinions upon subjects of which the writers thereof, are partially or wholly ignorant.

No better illustration of this can be afforded than by the word "Talisman," derived from the Greek verb "teleo," which means, primarily, to accomplish, or bring into effect. But, in its real, and therefore higher, sense, it means to dedicate, consecrate, and initiate into the arcana of the temple mysteries. But, in the present day it means a piece of imposture, connected with some magical hocus pocus of the ignorant and superstitious mind, a vulgar charm, that is supposed to bring the owner thereof some material benefit, irrespective of his mental, magnetic, and moral condition, "and," says the learned Webster, after describing his idea of such things, "they consist of three sorts, astronomical, magical and mixed." But in what sense the "astronomical" differed from the "magical" we are not informed, nor is any light thrown upon the peculiar nature of that class designated as "mixed." In fact, the lexicographer so mixes up his definitions that, we are unable to distinguish anything in particular, but his own individual ignorance.

So it has become, in every branch of learning. Words and their meanings have become so mixed in their use and application, that, the world is full of discords and misunderstandings, which lead into dissensions and contention, among all schools of thought, sects, and isms; and lastly, though not the least serious, it has reached into the close relations of the human family.

All writers and speakers, as well as the readers and listeners, should acquaint themselves with the derivation and meaning of words.

The fact stands very clearly defined that, Talismans are confused in the minds of the present generation with magical charms, which depend for their effects, upon the power of the idea or thought, which the formulating magician impresses upon the substance of which they are composed. If the magical artist be expert, and endowed with an exceedingly potent will, his charm may become very powerful, when worn by the person for whom it was prepared. But, if this one grand essential be lacking, no amount of cabalistical figures and sacred names will have any effect, because, there can be no potency in symbols apart from the ideas and mental force they are capable of arousing in the mind of the maker. Solomon's Seal is no more powerful, when drawn upon virgin parchment, with a weak will, or in a mechanical state of mind, than a child's innocent scribbling upon its slate. But, if the artist realizes the mysteries symbolized by the interlacing triangles, and can place his soul en rapport with the invisible elements they outwardly represent; then, powerful effects are often produced.

I am sorry to say that, the knowledge of charms is not confined to the creation of beneficial talismans. Its perversion has led to the diabolical practices of the Voodo and Black Magician, whose work is wholly, either for gain or revenge. Nothing, but the most extreme selfishness lies beneath such immoral practices, but, as there must be a light to reflect a shadow, so a charm must follow a talisman. Magical charms, then, are simply natural objects, possessing but little active virtue in themselves, but, owing to the mediumistic nature of their substances, are endowed with artificial powers, of temporary duration, by virtue of the idea and thought impressed upon them, through the mental magic of the maker; and in this sense, a charm must be clearly distinguished from "teleo," the Talisman. The very names suggest their difference, and, above all other men, students in Occultism should strive to become thoroughly educated in the true sense of the term, *men of letters,* by virtue of (as Ruskin calls it) "the kingship of words." "Charm" is derived from the Latin "carmen," a song that fascinates, and means to control by incantation, to subdue; while Teleo concerns the secret powers and wisdom of consecration and initiation. It is because of modern misuse of antique terms that, we have considered this somewhat lengthy explanation necessary, in order to clear away the accumulated debris of the ages, from the true foundation of our present study.

A Talisman is a natural object, containing the elemental forces of its own degree of life, in a state of intense activity, and capable of responding to the corresponding quality of life, *outside of itself,* that emanates from the same spiritual state, either by sympathetic vibration or antagonistic currents, the nature, power, quality, and degree of life, which the various natural objects represent, being a part of the temple curriculum of initiation. Hence, the name, by which the latent power of these natural objects became known, was in strict harmony with the facts involved.

In order to prevent any possible misconception upon the subject, let us briefly restate the definition in a different way: A Talisman is the exact antipodes of a charm. This latter is the artful and temporary result of man's mental power; the former, the natural production of universal Nature, and as permanent and enduring as the substance of which it is composed, *during the present cycle.* And yet in some sense, it may be quite correct to say that, a Talisman *acts like a charm,* and vice versa, that charms *act like a Talisman,* providing that, the real vital difference between them, is maintained in the statement.

Now that we have our subject clearly defined, let us carefully examine *how and in what sense* a given natural object becomes Talismanic, for it must appear self-evident to all that, one and the same substance cannot constitute a Talisman for everyone, and for everything. They must naturally differ, as widely in their nature and quality, as mankind differ in physical, mental, moral, ethical, and temperamental, development. And, yet, though, man may so differ from his fellow man; the ignorant Esquimau, killing seals in his kayak, may belong to the same spiritual quality of life as the Harvard professor, who obtains his subsistence by daily discourse upon the sublime harmony of the infinitely small with the infinitely great, throughout the manifested universe of matter, and wherever we find this *kinship* of the spirit, we shall find the same identical Talisman acting alike upon each, whenever they shall come en rapport with it. Mental, moral, and physical development, never alter the real nature of the internal man. Culture only brings to the surface, into active use, the latent possibilities lying concealed within the human soul. It only allows him to exercise his functions upon different planes, and with different effect.

Every natural department of Nature corresponds to some peculiar specific quality and degree of life. These have been divided, for the sake of convenience, into four primary groups; and each group again subdivided into three, corresponding to the four cardinal, four succedent, and four cadent houses, of the astrological chart; therefore, the twelve signs of the Zodiac; these constituting the Cycle of Necessity within physical conditions, wherein, the ever-measuring or decreeing tidal flow of life from solar radiation throughout the year, represents the twelve groups of humanity, of lower animated Nature, of vegetation, and crystallized gems. Every human being is ushered into the world under the direct influx of one or more of these celestial divisions, and by virtue of the sign occupying the horizon at the moment of birth, absorbs such influx, and becomes endowed with a specific polarity, by virtue of which, he ever afterward, during such expression within physical conditions, inspires with every breath, that specific life quality from the atmosphere, corresponding to the same degree of the universal spirit. Consequently, that gem, or those gems, representing and corresponding to *his House of Life,* become to him, a Talisman, because of their relationship—their spiritual affinity. These are all given in the second part of Vol. I. *The metals* never become Talismanic, because of their comparatively negative degree of life, and for this reason also, they make the most powerful charms. Certain combinations of metals, and in proper proportions, increase the potency and magnetic influence of a charm; and here, too, the laws of antipathy and affinity come into practical use.

A true expert will know his metals, or metal, and his client, before commencing his magical work.

Those persons who derive most virtue from a Talisman are those who belong to the most sensitive, or interior state, within such degree of life, and who are dominated by one sign only. Thus, if we find one sign occupying the whole of the House of Life, or practically so, as when the first face of a sign ascends, we may be sure, other things not interfering, that such a native will receive great benefit from wearing its Talismanic gem. If a person of good intellectual powers and sensitive spirituality, be born when the lord of the ascendant occupies the *rising sign*, as, for instance, Mars in Aries, or Sun in Leo, we may be sure that, the Talismanic gem, in their case, will be exceedingly powerful, because, all the Astro-physical conditions are then most favorable for the expression of natural forces, and, if worn upon, or near that part of the body which the sign rules, the power and influence is more powerful and beneficial.

In wearing them, take them to you as a part of yourself, a part of your higher self, a thing to be heeded, listened to and obeyed. They will usually make their presence most pronounced when something arises to disturb the harmonious vibrations that naturally and quietly go on between the person and the interstellar spaces above. They are like the sensor and motor nerves—they never make their presence known, except, when danger encroaches.

Having explained in what sense gems become talismanic, we have now to disclose the modus operandi—*the how*.

The gems contain the life quality of their own astral nature. Man, as a higher expression, only, of the same universal biune life, contains the same. Like two electric currents, *man, the positive pole* (comparatively), attracts unto himself *the mineral life of the gem*, which thus, becomes the negative pole. A complete circuit is formed and maintained, as long as they remain in contact. Gems belonging to a different quality of life, not being en rapport with his astral state, have no good effect, because, no current flows between them. Thus, the Talisman acts in unison with the psychic, or soul-principle, of man, aiding the organism to sustain health, stimulating the mental perceptions, and spiritual intuition, and affording in a remarkable manner, many premonitions of coming danger, when the individual is sufficiently sensitive to perceive them. And now, per contra, as there are gems that act in sympathy with man, there must be, and in fact are, gems that act upon contrary principles; i.e., antagonistic, and these belong to purely antagonistic elements, as Air to Earth and Fire to Water, unless the native be born under *both* forces, as Mars in Cancer (♋) rising, or the latter part of one sign and nearly the whole of another of an opposite nature, occupying the ascendant. Such natives are pure neutrals, and such might wear the gems that belong to the most powerful planet of the horoscope, or that triplicity holding the most planets; then, they are usually combined, the planet and the triplicity.

There are, of course, innumerable substances, more or less, capable of talismanic virtue to particular individuals. But those gems, and similar ones, that are given in "The Light of Egypt," Vol. I, are the most powerful. To these may be added the opal, under Scorpio (♏); the garnet, under Aries (♈); and the turquoise, under Cancer (♋), when Saturn is therein; and the aquamarine, under Pisces (♓); and among the temporary talismans of vegetation we may add that, the young shoots, bearing the flower and seed vessels, are the portions of chief virtue, and the young shoots of trees. These are often used in locating mines, wells, oils, etc., that lie hidden beneath the surface of the earth, and in the hands of a negative, sensitive person, seldom fail to reward the searcher with success. These should always be gathered when their ruling correspondences are rising, or, *better still, culminating upon the meridian.* These will be explained in the chapter on The Magic Wand.

We have now reached the limits of our present study, and have only to state that all gems, like the human organism, are in one of three conditions: alive and conscious, asleep and *unconscious,* or dead and powerless. These conditions can only be discovered, in stones, by the trained lucid or the instructed neophyte. Stones that are sleeping require to be awakened. This, also, can only be done by the trained student or Adept. Those that are dead, are *useless* as Talismans, no matter how beautiful they appear as ornaments.

Gems and stones are also sexed, and those who wear them would receive the best effect if they should wear those of opposite sex, although either is powerfully potent in their influence upon the individual. How very ignorant the children of men are, of the subtle, silent, yet obedient servants, that everywhere, surround them. Here, again, that Divine spark, which lies embedded within the crystallized forces of Nature, is exerting its subtle, spiritual influence, in making man's very selfishness, and love of ornament and show, a means, to bring forth these silent monitors, knowing ere long that, their true power and potency will be known, and consciously utilized by him, as potent factors in his soul's evolvement and physical development.

The twelve representative gems within the cold stratas of matter, stand as the material representatives of their stellar counterparts in the sky, and constitute the beautiful, glittering, but crystallized, Zodiac of man's physical anatomy.

CHAPTER X

CEREMONIAL MAGIC

The above title has been selected, chiefly, because, in most works treating upon magic we find it wrongly used, and therefore, take the opportunity of explaining the matter, for, there were no such terms in the vocabulary of the ancient Magi.

It is unfortunate, that, words of ancient origin are not more carefully used, and that, we should attach so many different meanings to the same word. The terms "ceremony" and "ceremonial" are nothing more nor less than, what that eminent critic, John Ruskin, would designate as "bastards of ignoble origin," which, somehow or another, have usurped the places of "rite" and "ritual." The word "rite" has descended to us from the Latin "ritus" of our Roman ancestors, and they received it from the more ancient "riti" of the Sanskrit, the Greek equivalent of which is "reo," and means the method or order of service to the gods, whereas, "ceremony" may mean anything and everything, from the terms of a brutal prize fight to the conduct of divine service within the church. But, no such chameleon-like definition or construction can properly be placed upon the word "rite," for it means distinctly, if it means anything at all, the serious usage and sacred method of conducting service in honor of the gods, or of superiors, and requires the attendance of the prophet or priest, or some one duly qualified to fulfill such sacred functions for the time being. The ritual of magic, then, is the correct title of this present study, and as such, we shall, henceforth, term it as we proceed with the course.

Man is especially, and above all creatures, an organizing force, and when to this fact, we add the most interior and powerful of his sentimental instincts—veneration for the powers that be, and for the higher, invisible forces of Nature, his "religiosity," as it has been aptly termed, we cannot wonder that, the earliest races of which we possess any record are chiefly distinguished for their imposing and elaborate religious rites. In fact, it is to the stupendous temples and a colossal sacerdotalism, that, we are indebted for nine-tenths of the relics and records which we possess of them. So true is this that, from what we have been able to discover, we are quite justified in asserting that the ancient races were, above all other things, a profoundly religious people. The temple was the center around which revolved all their genius and art, and the sacred edifice became their grandest achievement in architecture, and its high priest the most powerful individual in the state. In fact, it was in consequence of the real power invested in such sacred office that it was so intimately connected with the throne, and why royalty so frequently belonged to the priesthood or exercised priestly functions. And there can be no real doubt, but that, amongst the pastoral and more spiritual races of Earth's earliest inhabitants, the priest, by reason of his superior wisdom, was the first law-giver; and, by virtue of his sanctity of person and elevation of mind became their first, primitive king, a patriarchal monarch, whose scepter and symbol of power was the shepherd's peaceful crook; just as among the ruder nomads of the inhospitable North, we find the greatest hunters invested with the dignity of chief, whose significant symbol and scepter of royalty, upon their Nimrod thrones, was the trusty, successful spear. And the times in which we live have had their full effect upon these symbols, so significant of rule. The monarch has transformed the spear into the less harmful mace, while the Church has added an inch of iron to the crook. Therefore, the former has become less war-like, and the latter less peaceful, and, verily, in actual life we find them so.

The patriarchal sire, head of the tribal household, was the original priest; and the hearthstone the first altar around which the family rites were performed; and from this pure and primitive original have been evolved, through progressive ages, the stately temple and the sacred person of the despotic pontiff; from the sincere prayer the pure aspirations of the human heart and the joyous offerings of fruits and flowers to the invisible powers around them; and from the souls of their beloved ancestors has arisen the costly and complicated ritual of theology. And, if the theologians of to-day really knew the lost, secret meaning of their complicated rituals, and the unseen powers lying behind their external symbols, their anxieties for the continued life of their dying creeds would be turned to new hopes and faith, which could be demonstrated to their equally blind followers; that, that which they were teaching they knew, and could practically use the knowledge given forth in their sanctuaries; and, instead of offering up their supplications to an imaginary, personal Deity, their words, rites, and ceremonies, would take on the form and power that such should command, and they would become truly, what their title really means, a doctor of the soul. Then could they, intelligently, lead and direct the souls of their followers to the path of Christ (Truth), which leads up to salvation; not a vicarious atonement, but gaining the at-one-ment through the individual soul's development to a conscious relation, to that Divine spirit, we call God, where it can say "I know."

Out of those simple gifts, which were the spontaneous offerings of loving remembrance and unselfish charity, have grown the prayers, penances, sacrifices, and servile worship, of sacerdotalism. Out of the paternal consideration and love of the aged sire has evolved the haughty, chilling pride of the selfish, isolated priest, and which reflects its baneful influence upon the worshipers at their feet. They have also changed their once sacred, faithful, and reverent, obedience into suspicion and distrust, and with the educated to utter disgust. The light has been extinguished, and priest and people alike are groping about in darkness.

It is strange, yea, passing strange, the amount of human ignorance and folly that is revealed. When we look upon this picture and then upon that, verily we cannot help but ask the question, is mankind really progressing? We know that it is; we are keenly alive to the truth that the Anthem of Creation sounds out "Excelsior"—"move on," but how, and in what way (*spiritually*) we fail to comprehend. The cyclic development of the human soul is an inscrutable mystery.

All the considerations above presented must be thoroughly weighed and understood in order to arrive at the true value of "the dogma and ritual of high magic," as Eliphas Levi terms it; because, amid the vast array of tinselled drapery, the outcome of man's vain conceit and bombastic pride, we shall find very little that can be considered as vital and really essential to the rites of magic. The show, the drapery, the priestly ornaments and instruments, are to the really spiritual Occultist, but, as sounding brass and a tinkling cymbal. That they had, and still have, their legitimate uses, is true, but these uses do not concern magic, per se, nor its manifold powers. They awed the popular mind, and impressed upon the masses a due reverence for the powers that be. They were instrumental in holding the untrained passions of the common herd in check, by a wholesome fear of summary vengeance from the gods, so that this pageantry of magic, the outward priestly show, was more of a politic development than a spiritual necessity, an astute but, philosophical method of enabling the educated few to govern the uneducated many. And it was only when the educational and initiatory rites of the temple became corrupt, and the priest became the persecuting ally of the king—when, in real fact, the priest lost his spirituality in the desire for temporal power and place, that the people began to disbelieve his professions and rebel against his tyrannical control.

The powers that be, are now wielding their sword of justice, and unfurling the knowledge of freedom and truth to the aspiring mind of man. He has begun to feel his bondage and the yoke of oppression. The words of promise and love, instead of lifting him up to the God he has been taught to worship, bow him down in slavish obedience to his priest. Mankind cannot remain in this mental and spiritual darkness much longer. Already I see the break of day, the dawn of a new life, a new religion; or, rather, the re-establishing of the true, which is as old as Time itself. There is but One Law, One Principle, One Word, One Truth and One God.

The original requirements for the office of priest, and the rites of magic, were, as shown, a primitive, i.e., pure mind; one that had outgrown the lusts and passions of youth, a person of responsibility and experience; and even to this day the priest of the Roman Church is called by the familiar title of "father." And as Nature does not alter her laws and requirements in obedience to the moral development of the race, we may rest assured that the same requirements, of ten thousand years ago, still hold good to-day. You may enter your magic circle, drawn with prescribed rites, and you may intone your consecrations and chant your incantations; you may burn your incense in the brazen censer and pose in your flowing, priestly robes; you may bear the sacred pentacles of the spirit upon your breast and wave the magic sword to the four quarters of the heavens; yea, you may even do more—you may burn the secret sigil of the objurant spirit; and yell your conjurations and exorcisms till you are black in the face; but all in vain, my friend—all in vain. It will prove nothing but vanity and vexation of spirit unless the inward self, the soul, interblends with the outward Word, and contacting by its own dynamic intensity— the elemental vibrations of Nature—arouses these spiritual forces to the extent of responding to your call. When this can be done, but not until then, will your magical incantations have any effect upon the voiceless air. Not the priestly robes nor magic sword, not the incantations, *written word*, nor mystic circle, can produce Nature's response to Occult rite; but the fire of the inward spirit, the mental realization of each word and mystic sign, combined with the conscious knowledge of your own Deific powers—this, and this only, creates Nature's true magician.

Who and where can such be found? Are they so few that the echo answers back "Where and who?" Yet, there are many such upon the Earth at the present time, but the present mental conditions forbid them making their identity known. They would not be recognized and accepted as the *true* teachers, but reviled and persecuted and dubbed as insane. But silently, they are sowing the seed of truth that will spring up and bear fruit, where and when least expected.

Because evil is so active, truth is not lying dormant. The spirit of God, that Divine spark of Deity within every human soul, never sleeps, never rests. "On and upward" is its cry. "Omnia vincit veritas."

The grand sublimity of man's conception of at-one with the Infinite Father, at-one with the limitless universe of being, at-one with, and inheriting, all the sacred rights and inalienable prerogatives of the ineffable Adonai of the deathless soul, is the only test of man's qualification for the holy office; for, as Bulwer Lytton has truthfully said, "the loving throb of one great *human heart* will baffle more fiends than all the magicians' lore." So it is with the sacred ritual. One single aspirational thought, clearly defined, outweighs all the priestly trappings that the world has ever seen.

The success of all incarnations depends upon the complete unison of *voice* and *mind*, the interblend of which, produces the dynamic intonation, that chords with the inward rhythmic vibrations of the soul. Once this magical, dynamic, vibration is produced, there immediately springs into being the whole elemental world belonging thereto, by correspondence. Vocalists who hold their audiences spellbound do so by virtue of the magical vibrations they produce, and are in reality practical, even though unconscious, magicians. The same power, to a degree, lies in the voice when speaking, the graceful movement of the hand when obeying the will, and the eye rays forth the same dynamic power and becomes magical in its effects.

These powers are exercised more upon the physical plane, and no better illustration can be given, than, the power man is able to exert over the animal when gazing into its eyes.

Here, as well as in incantations and invocations, within the power of the will, lies the success or failure.

At this point it may be asked, what, then, is the use of magical rites, of symbols and priestly robes? We answer, in themselves alone, nothing, absolutely nothing, except the facility and convenience we derive from system, order and a code of procedure. To this may be added the mental force and enthusiasm of soul which such things inspire, just as men and women may feel more dignified, artistic, and refined, when dressed in accordance with their ideas. So may the average priest feel more priestly, holy; and consequently, more powerful mentally; when arrayed in the robes of his office and surrounded by the outward symbols of his power and functions. But, in themselves alone, there is not, nor can there be, any real virtue. The same may be said of the incantations. The words used in their composition are the hieroglyphics of mystical ideas. Therefore, the correct pronunciation of the words or the grammatical construction of a sentence is nothing, if the underlying idea is conceived in the mind and responded to by the soul. Will and motive form the basis of true magic.

One word more and we have completed our subject. Magic swords, rings, pentacles, and wands, may, and often are, powerful magical agents in the hands of the magician, by virtue of the power, or charm, that is invested within them when properly prepared; but apart from such preparation, by those *who know*, they are as powerless as unintelligible incantations.

All the foregoing are aids, but if physical manifestations of magical forces be required, there must always be present the necessary vital, magnetic pabulum, by means of which such phenomena are made to transpire; and in every case, to be successful, the assistance of a good natural magician, or seer, is necessary; for without this essential element the whole art, in its higher aspects, becomes abortive.

CHAPTER XI

This is the last lesson of our present course that requires a clear definition of the terms employed in the title thereof, for the twelfth, and final study is, perhaps, fortunate in having for its title a word that has not, so far, been misused and distorted from its original sense.

The Magic Wand. The words savor of everything that the young tyro in Occult art can picture to his mind; of the midnight magician and his mysterious, if not diabolical, arts, muttering his incantations, working his gruesome spells, and raising the restless ghosts of the dead. Strange fancies, these, and yet, so corrupt and ignorant have become the conceptions of the popular mind regarding the once sacred Science of the Temple and the psychological powers of Nature, that we very much question, if the ideas above stated were not very similar to the originals of each modern student, before he had become acquainted with the deeper truths—the realities of Occult philosophy.

We will commence our study by a careful investigation of the original meaning of the words Magic Wand, since those who were the masters and originators thereof, are far more likely to know more about them than their degenerate offspring of a later age. Few, comparatively, would believe that the words *magic, mason,* and *imagination,* are the present unrelated descendants of the same original conception—*the root idea;* but such is the case. First, then, we will examine their modern meanings. Magic is the unholy art of working secret spells, of using invisible powers, and holding intercourse with the unseen world of ghosts and demons, by means of enchantments. It also means the expert deception of the senses by the tricks of a conjurer, *so-called* hocus-pocus and fraud, and a magician is either an evil-minded, superstitious mortal, fool enough to believe in charms, or an expert pretender and imposter of the first water, who cheats and deceives the people. A mason is the honorable designation of a builder, who works in stone; metaphysically, a member of a semi-secret society, whose sole advantage is social intercourse and standing; who proclaim fraternity and universal brotherhood theoretically and practice the reverse in reality; a man who apes the Egyptian Mason, knows nothing in reality of Hiram, his master; who knows nothing of the starry Solomon or his mystic temple in the heavens, which Hiram built; and who misconceives the import of the three villains, or assassins; and who, further, knows nothing of that wonderful sprig of myrtle:—in short, a Free Mason, speaking generally, is a man who delights in ideals, social equality, secret fraternity, and plays at mysticism; who parades on the Masonic stage and enacts a role he does not understand. The first meaning, that of a builder, is the most correct. Lastly, the imagination is the exercise of mental imagery—the picturings of silent thought.

And now we will proceed *backwards*. Imagination is from the word "image," a form, a picture, and has descended to us from the Latin "imago," which, in its turn, was derived from the old Semitic root, "mag." Mason comes to us from the Latin "mass," which means to mould and form, i.e., to build; and the word "mass," through various transformations, was also derived from the root-word "mag." Consequently, originally, there was but little difference in the ancient idea of building pictures in the mind and erecting the mental idea externally in stone. It is from this fact, that, we have to-day *Mental Masons,* a la the secret orders, and stone masons, who labor for wages. The Mental Masons have merely lost the knowledge of their art. They should, by rights, be as active and correspondingly useful to-day as their more physical brothers, the masons of stone.

This art would never have fallen into disgrace and disuse, if their daily bread, or material accumulations, had depended upon their efforts in building up the mental, moral, and spiritual attainments, of each other, and bringing their knowledge into more external use, by making the material edifice, the physical body, a purer and more fitting temple, for the Divine soul.

Magic comes from the Latin "magi" and the Greek word "magos," which means wise, learned in the mysteries, and was the synonym of wisdom. The initiated philosopher, the priest, and the wise men, are all of them included in the "magi." Again, tracing this word to its remote ancestor, we find it terminating in the same Semitic root, "mag," but of this strange root no one was able to say much, except that it seemed to belong to the Assyrian branch of the great Semitic race. But quite recently, thanks to our scientific explorers and archaeologists, versed in the mysterious meaning of cuniform inscription; Assyrian scholars now inform us that they have found the hoary, primitive original of it, of magic, magi and imago, etc. It is from an old Akkadian word, "imga," meaning wise, holy, and learned, and was used as the distinguishing title of their wisest sages, priests, and philosophers, who, as may be supposed, gradually formed a peculiar caste, which merged into the ruling priestly order. The Semites, who succeeded the old Akkadian race in the valley of the Euphrates, as a mere matter of verbal convenience, transformed many of the old Akkadian words to suit their own articulation, and "imga" became "mag," and thus "magi." *The blend* between the Semetic and the older Akkadian race, produced, by fusion of racial blood, the famed Chaldeans. So that we see how old are the words which many of us daily use, but with different meaning. Verily, it makes one feel, when he thinks of magic and its origin, as though he were quite nearly related to the people who honored King Sargon, the Wise, the earthly original of the mystic Solomon of Biblical tradition. The term Wand is an old Saxon word, which primarily signifies to set in motion, to move. From this we derive our word wander, i.e., to roam, and wandering, i.e., moving and continually restless.

We have now the original, therefore real, meaning of the words Magic Wand; thus an object that sets in motion the powers of the magician, and the magician, an Initiate of the sacred rites—*a master of wisdom,* possessing all the resources that enable him *to build,* mould, and form; to create in fact, by virtue of his knowledge of the secret powers of mental imagery and the potential use of his own imagination. He is both Mental Mason and learned philosopher.

The student may doubtless ask, why all this care and labor regarding mere definitions? We reply that, it is because, the real meaning of the words we have purposely selected for the title of our studies are, in themselves, a far better revelation than we could possibly have written. Originally, ideas and words were related as absolute expressions or correspondences, of each other. This is not so now. As the different races became interblended, the purity of both language and morals retrograded, and the people grew more to the external. The intuitions and spirit were compelled to retreat, giving place to only the intellectual and mental. The blending of the languages gave birth to many words wherein different meanings were transmitted; hence, the trouble arising to-day over the numerous interpretations of a single word.

Hybrid races have no such thing as a pure language. Their ideas and language, like their blood, is badly mixed up, confusing, and unsatisfactory, so far as the real meaning of the words are concerned. For this very reason we find so many different meanings for the same word; and also for this reason, we cannot formulate a legal enactment in the Anglo-Saxon tongue that, a learned lawyer, versed in this senseless jugglery of words, cannot demonstrate, to the satisfaction of the courts, means something the very opposite of the real intentions—the spirit—which the framers thereof, intended it to convey. Anciently, it required no artful cunning of the lawyer to interpret the laws. The words had only one simple and obvious meaning. If a language could be so constructed to-day, and the antiquated precedents of the courts annihilated; the legal profession would be exterminated inside of twelve months, and an affliction removed from the people.

The philosophy of the Magic Wand is this. It is a magnetic, electric conductor for the magician's will. It directs the flow of his thought and concentrates it upon a given point in space or an object. It is, magically, what the sights of a rifle are to a sportsman. It enables him to focus his powers with exact precision upon the mark against which, or upon which, his will is directed. Apart from this there is no power, per se, in the Wand itself, any more than there is in a lightning conductor without the electric storm. Ergo, the Wand is the conductor, in the magician's hand, for the lightnings of the soul; and just as the lightning rod is most useful and most powerful to protect, when the storm is the strongest; so is the Wand most powerful in the hands of the most potential magician. We can only transmit through this Wand the degree of force we may happen to possess in the soul.

In a properly prepared Wand lies the most powerful weapon, to protect or destroy, that can be placed within a magician's hands. With his own spiritual force and knowledge, combined with the magic power attached to the instrument, nothing can withstand its power, when directed with a determined and powerful will.

Many substances have been employed in the manufacture of these Magic Wands. Metals or stones will not serve this purpose, unless covered with some organic matter. In any case stones are worthless. The very finest Wands are made from the live ivory of a female elephant. A short Wand, twenty-one inches long, tipped with gold at the largest end and silver or copper at the other, is very powerful.

Next to these costly articles are Wands with a gold or copper core, a wire, in fact, cased with ebony, boxwood, rosewood, cedar or sandal-wood. English yew also serves the purpose; so does almond wood. Simpler, less expensive, and almost as effective, are Wands made of witch-hazel. In fact, apart from the Wands of live ivory, I consider that witch-hazel is as powerful as the golden Wand. Next in force to this witch-hazel are the shoots of the almond tree, and, lastly, the peach and swamp willow.

The proper time to manufacture a Magic Wand is whenever you can find the person who is able to do the work. But after it is constructed it must be thoroughly magnetized, with proper ceremony and aspiration, the first or the second full Moon after the Sun enters Capricorn, at midnight, when the Moon will be culminating in her own sign upon the mid-heaven.

The best time *to cut* a shoot of witch-hazel or other material for a Wand is the first full Moon after the Sun's entry into Capricorn, at midnight, and then magnetize it upon the next full Moon at the same hour.

In conclusion, let us repeat that, the Magic Wand is but the highly sensitive magical medium for transmitting and concentrating the force of the learned magician; that it is equally powerful under great excitement of mind, *whether used consciously or not.* The stream of mental fire will go in the direction the Wand happens to be pointed, and, therefore, should never be in the hands of the wicked or foolish, any more than firearms. It is potential or otherwise, in exact proportion to the artist's wisdom and dynamic mentality, and is useless in the hands of the idiotic or weak-minded. A Magic Wand requires brains and vigorous mental force to make it effective, just as the steam engine requires an apparatus for generating the steam, that moves it. With a determined will, and a mental conception of one's inward power, any man or woman can, by means of this sensitive Wand, defy all the legionaries of Hell, and quickly disperse every form of spiritual iniquity.

The firearms which have become so intricate in their mechanism and so destructive in their operations, are only a degeneration of the Magic Wand. The first weapons of warfare and slaughter were very crude and clumsy, then larger and more destructive, until at last they have become as fine in texture and mechanical genius, compared with their early brothers, as the Magic Wand is to-day, above and beyond, the present weapons of warfare. At last, the original mode of defense will be rediscovered and become a utility in the hands of the majority of mankind. At the same time, the mental and moral nature will be evolving into better conditions, too, so that their use will not be given to the ignorant and evildoers, but placed in charge of the educated, those who are morally capable of leading and ruling.

Yes, we are now stepping upon the plane of reason and intuition, where right, not might, will prevail and rule the world. · The present mode of government and rule will be changed, and one of humanitarian justice take its place.

God hasten the Millenium.

CHAPTER XII

THE BOOK
WHICH IS CALLED
THE TABLETS OF ÆTH

THE SACRED SCROLL WHICH IS CALLED

THE TABLETS OF ÆTH

Now FOR THE FIRST TIME TRANSCRIBED FROM THE

ASTRAL RECORDS AND DONE INTO A BOOK,

IN THREE PARTS.

By ZANONI, ⫫

TO WHICH IS ADDED A SERIES OF INTERPRETATIVE REFLECTIONS

FOR THE SPIRITUAL MEDITATION OF THE FAITHFUL.

FOREWORD

Thy temple is the arch
Of yon unmeasured sky;
Thy Sabbath the stupendous march
Of grand eternity.

To my Brothers and Sisters of the Hermetic Brotherhood of Luxor:

GREETING—For some years it has been my desire to leave a spiritual legacy to the many devoted friends and followers who have braved so much amid present truth and error for my sake.

In choosing the present work for such a purpose, I have had in view the deeper spiritual needs of the soul—the prophetic element of the interior spirit, which can best exalt itself through the contemplation of Nature's arcane symbolism of the starry heavens—not the material expression of the glittering splendors of the midnight sky, but the spiritual soul-pictures of those blazing systems that reveal to the seeing eye the shining thrones of *the Rulers*—the Powers that Be.

Ever since the dawn of intellectual human life upon our Mother Earth, long before the days of the cave man, or even the first frost that heralded the coming of the Ice Age, souls have hoped and hungered and souls have quailed and fallen in their struggles with the mysteries of God. But ever and anon some bright flower of the race has gained the spiritual victory. A Messianic soul has responded to aspirations of a great-hearted, great-souled woman, pregnant with spiritual yearnings beyond her race, and she has unconsciously blessed her kind for the generations yet to come with that incarnated mystery—*the Son of God.* Blessed, O Woman, is thy patient mission on the earth, and transcendent are the holy mysteries of thy maternity. Every human birth is a Divine miracle in humanity, performed by the Motherhood of God.

Hence it is that, from the earliest ages of life, triumphant souls have stormed the gates of the sanctuary and penetrated Nature's most occult mysteries and there recorded their spiritual victories. Amid these sacred records lies one great scroll, that none but the brightest and bravest may read.

This sacred scroll, sealed with the seven mystic seals of the heavens, contains *The Tablets of Æth,* a record of the soul's experiences upon the planes of both conscious and sub-conscious life—spirit and matter, that are expressed in a series of universal symbols, which manifest to the seer the processes of creative life, of spiritual cause with material effect. And, finally, the mystery of the seven vials and the seven stars of Saint John are written therein; for the Tablets are the hieroglyphic keys which unlock the realities of truth involved within the unrealities of external life, and open up, to the aspiring soul, inconceivable vistas of knowledge yet possible of realization, within the Divine womb of the uncreated Æther.

Myriads of exalted spirits, who have toiled for the treasure which doth not corrupt, have added, and are adding, their portion of personal conception to this universal conception of life, so that the sacred symbols themselves, inscribed upon these imperishable Tablets, *are evolutionary*—are slowly unfolding through the eons of time, and revealing wider and yet deeper processes of the light, life, and love, of the Motherhood of God.

Therefore, all Divine revelation of infinite truth is limited and finite as to its conception, when revealed through a finite capacity. All Divine truths are universal; all personal conceptions of such truths are limited; hence springs the unquenchable fountain of the *one* eternal truth, enternally repeating itself, in cosmic as in human life, by the progressive unfoldment of Nature's unlimited potentialities.

> "The outward doth from the inward roll,
> And the inward dwells in the inmost soul."

The true poet is always a seer, and he might have added that the *inmost soul* is the uncreate, and, the yet uncreated itself, lies buried in the ever eternal beyond; hence the immortality of the human spirit.

This sacred astral scroll, rightly and reverently studied by the disciple of the higher law, becomes a boundless source of knowledge and inspiriation. There is no mood of the mind or yearning of the soul that cannot be satisfied and refreshed from this inexhaustible fountain of spiritual truth, no passion of the human heart that cannot be eased of its burden and soothed of its pain. Its spiritual refreshment falls like the dew from heaven upon those who are weary and heavy laden with the trials and sufferings of external life.

Accept it, then, even as it is given unto you. My friends and brethren, accept it as Zanoni's last work on earth—his legacy to you, and may the spirit of the All-Father-Mother, the ineffable spirit of Life, Light, and Love,—the Unknowable, whom men call God, rest upon you and be with you now and forever.

Very Truly
T. H. Burgoyne. ☉.

INTRODUCTION

To the Book Which Is Called "The Tablets of Æth," Wherein Are Described The Formulas of Meditation.

THE FORMULAS OF MEDITATION,

TO THE DRAGON, FOUNTAIN OF YOUTH.

"When first, a musing boy, I stood beside
Thy starlit shimmer, and asked my restless heart
What secrets Nature to the herd denied,
But might to earnest hierophant impart;
When lo! beside me, around and o'er,
Thought whispered, 'Arise, O seeker, and explore.' "

The Tablets of Æth are the culminating expression of symbolical ideas, and the studious meditation thereof is to be approached and continued in this wise:

First, commit to memory, as near as may be, all the ideas involved in the astrological laws and principles laid down in "The Science of the Stars," formulated in the second part of "The Light of Egypt," Vol. I, especially as regards the symbolism there given and manifestation thereof on the intellectual plane. Mentally digest these aspects of truth most thoroughly.

Second, carry forward the same course of mental training with regard to the preceding chapters in this volume, from No. 1 to No. 12. There are thirteen chapters, but No. 13, the last one, being "The Penetralia," should not be included in this course, but, rightly used, should be reserved as the last and final revelation for spiritual contemplation.

The twelve chapters just mentioned continue the great astral laws given in "The Light of Egypt," Vol. I, from this plane to that of the soul life of the human monad (both prior to and after human incarnation). At this point we leave the finite and step into the realms of the infinite. From the sphere of limitations which surround the microcosm we enter the starlit path of the macrocosm, and here, with the

illimitable ocean of eternal life sweeping onward before us, we hear
the first strains of the Grand March of the Universe burst forth from
the organs of God! The suns of creative life swell the infinite chorus
of sound; archangels swing their fiery batons to the march of the
heavenly host; and all earthly sound has ceased. We are absorbed
in the music of the spheres.

We are now in the realm of universals, the domain of living realities. The Tarot of Mother Nature revolves before us, revealing her
mystic meanings to the soul. All ideas are symbols, and symbols are
reservoirs for the conservation of thought. And this is a very truth:
Even so on earth as it is in heaven.

The Tablets of Æth, then, constitute a spiritual astrology, a spiritual science of the stars, void of mathematics, yet possessing all the
exactitude of figures, constructed on the principles of astronomy, yet
expressed by the methods of the Kabbalah.

The transmission of spiritual truth from inward to outward form,
though differing according to the age in which it is expressed, is ever the
same in principle. And in the same way that the sacred *clavicula* of
Solomon became the Tarot of Bohemian gypsies, so did the Tablets of
Æth manifest their mysteries in the starry science of Chaldean lore.
But there is this sharp line of demarcation between them, namely, the
Tablets of Æth deal with universal human life and nature, with infinite
principles from which all finite laws radiate. The Tablets of Æth
express and symbolize the cause. All other mundane systems of occult
study, astronomical or metaphysical, are spirito-natural effects, the
individual intellectual fruits, gathered from the one universal tree of
knowledge. Uncreated, Unlimited Potentiality, is the one impersonal
truth shining forever in the Great White Light of God. All the laws,
powers, and principalities, manifested in the moving Universe, are
but the colored rays, blazing with glorious life through the prisms of
matter.

Having stated thus much, the neophyte will perceive in what
meditative sphere of thought the Tablets may be used. The method
of study is, as shown, a purely synthetic deduction of human ideas
from spiritual symbols of universal principles. The Tablets themselves
constitute a grand arcane Tarot of man, God and the universe, and of
all the powers that dwell therein. They may be studied singly, as, for
instance, meditating upon some one great universal idea or principle;

or they may be studied in trines, as they appear in each separate book, or chapter, or as squares, like two, five, eight, eleven, or as the seal of two trines, one, three, five, seven, nine, eleven, with No. twelve in the center, as the revealer of the mystery. And, finally, they may be contemplated as the Grand Oracle of Heaven, in the following manner:

Make a circle of the tablets, as you would with a pack of Tarot cards, beginning with No. 1, ♈, on the eastern horizon, and proceeding in the exact opposite order from a figure of the heavens—No. 2, ♉, being on the Twelfth House, No. 3, ♊, on the Eleventh, and ♋ on the M. C. of the figure, as in the Astro-Masonic chart, given in the second part of "The Light of Egypt," Vol. I, and so proceed with the rest of the twelve tablets of the stars. This figure will represent the potentialities of the macrocosm, the starry signs symbolizing the possibilities of things past or to be, and the rulers the active executors thereof. Study the figure in all its aspects as such, first singly, tablet by tablet, then as a whole—the cosmos. Next, place the ruler of any given tablet at the side of the Mansion, and try to penetrate its various meanings, powers and possibilities. Then proceed the same with a trine and a square, and, last, with all the rulers, in the order of their celestial lordship of the signs, each in his appointed place, as a whole Arcana.

In any grave crisis of mental or physical affairs, wherein nations, and not individuals, are concerned, the tablets may be used as a celestial scheme of the heavens, thus: Cast a figure of the heavens for the Sun's first entry into the sign Aries at the vernal equinox, calculated for the meridian of the capital city of the country under consideration. Degrees and minutes are not wanted. Then place the twelve tablets in place of signs, exactly as they would occur in an astrological figure. Then place the rulers of the Sun, Moon and planets therein (each having its own tablet), as they are found to be situated in an ephemeris for the time of the figure. This done, study the whole from a spiritual standpoint as the causes and ultimates of the crisis, according to astro laws.

The foregoing simple directions will, I think, be sufficiently plain for all purposes, never forgetting that this holy study is not a system of divination, as commonly understood, but of Divine revelation, in its highest and most holy religious sense. Long study and most reverent meditation will be required to master this mystery, and many errors of judgment will occur to the beginner.

The interpretative reflections are added for the purpose of guiding and guarding the spiritually untrained seer from possible error in fundamental conceptions only. They must not by any means be taken as a complete revelation of the tablets, but only as a series of skeleton keys by means of which all things may be revealed to the earnest seeker thereof. To have added more than is given would only be to defeat the object of this work. Each seeker for the truth must excavate the mines of knowledge, and dig further into this universal well of truth for himself.

Remember that all interpretation will be personal to each student. Of no one can it be affirmed, "thou hast said," and so endeth the matter. Not so. To each, according to his talent, shall the mysteries of the kingdom be revealed, to every one according to his humility, spiritual light, and merit. But from the arrogant, the selfish, and spiritually proud, shall all things be taken away, and truth shroud herself in the veil of delusion. In simplicity of mind, then, and purity of soul, approach the Holy of Holies. "Suffer little children to come unto Me," saith a messenger of the Most High, "for of such is the Kingdom of Heaven." Verily, therefore, I say unto you, that not until you can look upon all the works of Nature—beauty in her nakedness or vice and crime in their repulsiveness, with pure thought and holy feeling, can you inherit eternal life.

Here endeth the introduction to the book which is called "The Tablets of Æth."

CHAPTER XII

PART I

of The Book which is called

THE TABLETS OF ÆTH

OF THE TWELVE MANSIONS

———

Here beginneth Chapter I of the Book which is called "The Tablets of Æth," wherein is transcribed the First Quadrant of the Twelve Mansions.

———

"I sent my soul through the invisible,
  Some lesson of that after life to spell;
  And by and by my soul returned to me
  And answered, 'I, myself, am Heaven and Hell.'"

———

"The moving finger writes; and, having writ,
  Moves on; nor all your piety nor wit
  Shall lure it back to cancel half a line,
  Nor all your tears wash out a word of it."

TABLET THE FIRST

Aries

♈

SYMBOL

—

A deep blue Sky, a blaze,

as if something were

about to rise.

I

REFLECTION

TABLET THE FIRST

The blush of dawn of a new life, all nature quivering with the sense of coming, conscious life; Isis, vibrant with love of the coming child, her bosom flushed in expectation of the little son soon to breathe on her yearning breast.

In this we trace the great lesson of preparation, of sending the light before the form, of the prophecy before the fulfillment. Dawn must precede sunrise. What you expect will be your destiny.

It is the longing of centuries that incarnates a god, a real Sun-God, whose vibrant love-life can thrill other lives into prayer—aspiration, the struggle for eternal life. The dawn represents the expectant maternity of Nature—God.

O child of Adam! See that thou expecteth much, and that thy aspirations are reflected in thy outward life.

TABLET THE SECOND

Taurus

♉

SYMBOL

———

A red sun

on the horizon

of

an inky sea.

II

REFLECTION

TABLET THE SECOND

Nature has shown forth her glory, as brought forth by young Horus, but her creative force is still unreflected. The sea is black and inky. The Son of God is born, but the sea of human life still remains unconscious, in primeval darkness.

The angles of the Sun and the sea are not yet in right relation to each other. A few, standing on the watch-towers of life, seeing the red glow of the risen sun, call "Look!" But the unfortunate ones in the outer darkness cry, as they beat their breasts; "No! There is no light! You do but dream!" And yet the Sun of Life has risen—the Divine light glows.

O child of Adam! Remember that "In Him was life, and life was the light of man, and the light shineth in the darkness, and the darkness comprehended it not."

TABLET THE THIRD

Gemini

♊

SYMBOL

———

Two stars are rising at
angles to each other and
to the Polar star,
while eight stars shine
faintly in the black space
of background. ★

★

★

III

REFLECTION

TABLET THE THIRD

The Divine symbol of soul-matehood is here signified in the two stars rising in the foreground; not only the soul-affinities of humanity, but the eternal father-mother forces manifested in the biune spirit of universal life and nature, the two great creative powers, Life and Light, whose harmony creates love, attraction and repulsion, and the straight lines of law and justice, which blend in the spiral of mercy.

The two stars are rising at an oblique angle to the pole-star, the center around which, material things revolve. So, too, life and love are balanced by the star of wisdom. Love in the spirit is adaption to the environment in matter and providence in universal life. The eight stars reveal the mystery of the tablet—universal death, present with life, the final end of all discord glimmers faintly afar off, and man questions the love of God, seeing that all things pass away, not realizing that death is the germinal promise of life, of transformation, of the realization of unrealized hopes, of the union of loving hearts in their starry pilgrimage back to the Father's home.

O child of Adam! Listen unto the words of the Teacher: "I and the Father are one." Suffer little children to come unto me, for of such is the Kingdom of Heaven."

PART I

———

Here beginneth Chapter 2 of the Book which is called "The Tablets of Æth," wherein is transcribed the Second Quadrant of the Twelve Mansions.

———

"How they struggle in the immense Universe!
How they whirl and seek!
Innumerable souls, that all spring forth
From the vast world-soul.
They drop from planet to planet,
And in the abyss they weep
For their forgotten land.
These are thy tears, O Dionysus,
O Spirit vast, Divine One, Liberator.
Draw back thy daughters to the breast of light."

———

"Ah, love! Could you and I with him conspire
To grasp this sorry scheme of things entire,
Would we not shatter it to bits? And then
Remould it nearer to the heart's desire."

TABLET THE FOURTH

Cancer

♋

SYMBOL

———

A woman's face

unconscious, in trance,

surrounded by

clouds.

IV

REFLECTION

TABLET THE FOURTH

The dreaming woman, whose brooding thoughts shape the coming man. The race is never any farther advanced than the average thought of the woman. She is yet sleeping, knowing not her powers. So, not until she awakes and recognizes herself as conceiving by the Holy Ghost and the mother of the incarnate God, will that God be brought forth unto universal knowledge.

In this is the great lesson to woman: Ever remember thy creative power as the mother of the humanity of the future. The sun in thy mansion exerts its highest power. Awake, therefore, O soul, and eclipse not its brightness with thy dreams of sublunary power.

O child of Adam! Ever honor the womb that gave thee birth, and know that all thy earthly greatness received its seed therefrom. A fountain cannot rise higher than its source.

TABLET THE FIFTH

Leo

♌

SYMBOL

———

A man's arm, bent,
exceedingly muscular,
a knife in the hand,
a streak of lightning
opposite the arm, which is
defying the lightning.

V

REFLECTION

TABLET THE FIFTH

Here we have the symbol of the incarnate fire of the spirit defying the mere natural fire of the heavens. The woman sleeps and broods and dreams, but the man she has brought forth is awake, and bids defiance to the fiery forces of Nature. He has armed himself with the keen knife of action, and with it has conquered the forces of matter. He has harnessed the lightning, and made the electric fluid his obedient slave. And thus has he mastered all forces inferior to spirit—that spirit of conscious life which is his birthright.

The lesson to be gleaned from this is that, the kingdom of Nature must be taken by storm. Not for rest, but for work, has Mother Nature sent forth her man child; not for peace, but for battle; not for inertia, but for effort.

O child of Adam! Arm yourself with the sword—mayhap the sword of affliction —and, gallantly raising the strong right arm aloft, hurl defiance at the chaos of Nature, sure that the fire from the Sun of the spirit is burning in every vein of that arm.

TABLET THE SIXTH

Virgo

♍

SYMBOL

———

A Lotus, rising from the

water, coiled around

its stem a snake,

whose efforts fail to reach

the flower.

VI

REFLECTION

TABLET THE SIXTH

Here we have the sacred flower, symbol of the virgin soul, uncontaminated by the snake of passion, which can only enfold the body—the stem; the snake of matter—of lust—of evil. But the flower of the spirit—the soul—lifts its pure white petals upward as an incense cup to the Sun of the Spirit.

In this symbol read the great lesson of the experience of evil. If, the flower of the soul, blossoms; the mud of the soil and the snake of the passions are but the surroundings of its roots and stem. Both are necessary for the perfection of the flower. The roots sink deep into Mother Earth, and draw nourishment and life, lifting matter upward, while the snake of passion becomes, under another aspect, the serpent of wisdom. Coiled around the stem of this life, it gives to the incarnated soul that wisdom which later blossoms in the Seraph of the Sun spheres.

O child of Adam! Take suffering, if it forge the sword of the spirit. Take evil and passion, and turn them into deep lessons of life, blossoming the evil into good, changing passion into wisdom. Only "the pure in heart can see God."

PART I

———

Here beginneth Chapter 3 of the Book which is called "The Tablets of Æth," wherein is transcribed the Third Quadrant of the Twelve Mansions.

————

"To know what really exists, one must cultivate silence with one's self, for it is in silence that the eternal and unexpected flowers open, which change their form and color according to the soul in which they grow. Souls are weighed in silence, as gold and silver are weighed in pure water."

————

"The worldly hope men set their hearts upon turns to ashes; or it prospers, and anon, like snow upon the desert's dusty face, lighting a little hour or two, is gone."

TABLET THE SEVENTH

Libra

≏

SYMBOL

———

A crowned king, with a
scythe raised in the
air, looks closely at two
boys wrestling
beneath him in a field of
grain, a red poppy
below them.

VII

REFLECTION

TABLET THE SEVENTH

The symbol of Nature's eternal war for the impossible equilibrium between spirit and matter; the symbol, also, of Time, which is but the illusion in which eternity clothes itself; forever putting on and forever putting off new garments of matter. The crowned king is the victorious soul, waiting, with the scythe of Time, to reap the harvest of the world; while incarnated man, as represented in the wrestling youths, is struggling for that which he did not produce, and which only death can reap. The poppy reveals the secret of the illusions of Nature's master-showman. All earthly things are unreal to the spirit, which is the only real thing. Man's effort to hoard and save the things of this world *is injustice to others*. The struggle is eternal, and no matter how careful or cunning man is to monopolize either power, truth or wealth, swift-footed time will readjust all things without error.

O child of Adam! "Lay not up for yourselves treasures upon earth, where moth and rust doth corrupt and where thieves break through and steal."

TABLET THE EIGHTH

Scorpio

♏

SYMBOL

———

A wide, arid plain, on it a
skeleton; a dull, grey sky,
in which an Eagle soars,
full-fed, it seems, from
the flesh of the skeleton.

VIII

REFLECTION

TABLET THE EIGHTH

A significant symbol to the seer, showing forth the two ultimates of life and death, of earthly things and sex. Scorpio is both the eagle of the spirit, soaring aloft, well fed with all that is worth carrying away from the earth; and also the scorpion, whose natural home is the desert.

In sex, either way, life is given. Shall it be to your spirit making fat and full your immortal self, or will the other interpretation be yours? And will you leave yourself dead and annihilated, a skeleton, to the Ego, the Divine spirit? For sex is indeed the foundation of all. Raised to the region of Libra, it is power and magnetism. To the bosom it is love; to the brain it is enthusiasm. It is the promethian fire of life, the creative force, giving vigor to whatever region to which it is raised; or, lowered, to be spent with no returns, it debases and renders life a desert of dry bones.

O child of Adam! Reflect on the fall of man from spirit to matter, and combine the wisdom of the serpent with the purity of the dove, and "lest ye partake of the tree of life ye shall surely die."

TABLET THE NINTH

Saggitarius

↗

SYMBOL

A child in a shell, holding
in its hand a feathered lance,
is drawn by five stars,
grouped in an under arc.

IX

REFLECTION

TABLET THE NINTH

The symbol of the conscious soul. The shell is the body, drawn by the five senses—stars—which form an under arc, to represent the world of material things and our relation thereto. The child, armed with the feathered lance, is the soul; riding thus, fully armed, in the shell of the body, it realizes the duality of truth; that all things are changeable; and that each thing is true upon the plane of its manifestation, while an illusion to that which is interior to its life, while the soul is in its dream state. Sagittarius represents conservatism and the permanence of crystallized institutions; but, when the spirit awakes and bursts the shell of matter, the senses, instead of being the guardians and jailors of its environment, become its servants, and the means by which, united as the one Ego, sense-perception, it races o'er the fields of Æth—a being of life and beauty, shining in the empyrean of God.

O child of Adam! Ever remember that temperament and environment constitute the north and south poles of human possibility, and that ability, combined with opportunity, is the measure of responsibility.

PART I

———

Here beginneth Chapter 4 of the Book which is called "The Tablets of Æth," wherein is transcribed the Fourth Quadrant of the Twelve Mansions.

———

"A hair, perhaps, divides the false and true.
Yes, and a single alif were the clue—
Could you but find it—to the treasure house,
And, peradventure, to *the Master*, too."

———

"Beware, O my son, of self-incense. It is the most dangerous on account of its agreeable intoxication. • • • Learn, O my beloved, that the light of Allah's truth will often penetrate an empty head more easily than one too crammed with learning."

TABLET THE TENTH

Capricorn

VS

SYMBOL

———

A deep, black ground,
o'er which shimmers a
phosphorescent light; at
each side an aurora
borealis rises, mountain like;
above all, a tiny star.

X

REFLECTION

TABLET THE TENTH

Here is revealed the symbol of the messenger of the Most High. The star hovers over the phosphorescent light cast on the darkness as the spirit hovers over the blackness of matter. The aurora borealis stands as the emblem for the magnetic attraction of Earth on spirit, the Christ soon to be born in the manger of the Goat; the descent of the Holy Ghost into material form, so that heavenly truth may illumine the drear speculum of earthly thought with the Divine iridescence of celestial light. It is the lowest arc of the cycle that reveals the new birth of death unto life—the divine egg of Brahma, containing the promise of the new law: "Peace on Earth, good will towards men."

O child of Adam! Be thou the star, and not a dweller of the outer darkness, and "Let your light so shine before men, that, they may see your good works."

TABLET THE ELEVENTH

Aquarius

~~~

SYMBOL

———

A stormy sea is seen;
above it the eight stars
shine, brilliant and
clear.

XI

REFLECTION

TABLET THE ELEVENTH

This tablet symbolizes the complete materialization of man—man, perfect on the earth and the lord thereof, in so far as material forces are concerned. The storm is the tempest of life, the whirl of the elements of matter in their battle with the spirit. The eight stars, brilliant now (for they are the same stars that were dimly seen in Gemini), show that the conquest of matter is complete, the great fall of spirit finished; the end of involution. And this would bring stagnation and death, if peace now ensued. The lesson taught is that, not in peace and rest can the soul grow; but amidst the earthquakes that shake thrones, the floods that overwhelm countries, the fires that reduce to ashes, has the strong man-soul grown to its present state and power. So fear not the storm, but the calm; not the unrest, but the quiet; fear not the battle, but the ignoble peace of the coward.

O child of Adam! The astral soul must learn to do and dare. Not over the brave man's grave shall it be written, "Rest in peace," but "I will arise, and go to my father."

TABLET THE TWELFTH

Pisces

♓

SYMBOL

———

A comet, beyond it infinite
things, only dreamed of
as yet, a world floating
in an ocean and in night,
beneath are two hands
clasped palm to palm.

XII

TABLET THE TWELFTH

A revelation of the to be. The comet is the twelfth Avatar, the herald, coming forth from the starry abyss of the infinite, staying with us a little while, and then flashing on his shining way to other worlds than ours, bearing *the Divine Word* from sun to planet, as the fiery messenger of God. And here the soul may well ask: "Who? Where? Whence and Whither?" For behold, he has come, and gone, and

> "Earth could not answer; nor the seas that mourn
> In flowing purple, of their Lord forlorn;
> Nor rolling Heaven, with all his signs revealed
> And hidden by the sleeve of night and morn."

The world floating in the sea of the infinite and resting in night shows the present state of humanity. But, "the blush of dawn" is ready to gladden the soul, and the expectant seer, from his lonely vigil on the hilltop, awaits the sunlight which will soon flood the world anew.

The two clasped hands point to many problems, chiefly soul-matehood, the message of the starry messenger, universal brotherhood, and the Father-Motherhood of God.

O child of Adam! Watch and pray, that a voice of the silence may speak unto you.

Here endeth the four Quadrants of the Tablets of the Twelve Mansions, wherein are revealed the signs and symbols thereof, as faithfully transcribed from the sacred roll in the astral records and called "The Tablets of Æth."

April, 1893.

CHAPTER XII

PART II

of The Book which is called

THE TABLETS OF ÆTH

———————

OF THE TEN PLANETARY RULERS

PART II

———

Here beginneth Chapter I of the Second Part of the Book which is called "The Tablets of Æth," wherein is transcribed the First Trinity of the Planetary Rulers.

———

"The human heart is the true temple of God; enter ye into your temples and illumine them with good thoughts. The sacred vessels, they are your hands and your eyes. Do I say that which is agreeable to God—doing good to your neighbors? But, first embellish wherein dwells He, who gave you life."

———

"How small soever your lamp be, never give away the oil which feeds it, but only the light and flame, which crown it."

TABLET THE FIRST

The Sun

⊙

SYMBOL

———

A flaming splendor,

a center of

light, radiating in all

directions.

I

REFLECTION

TABLET THE FIRST

The symbol of all created life, spiritual and material; of all goodness, human or Divine; the center of all thought, from brutal instinct to Deific wisdom; of all creations, from starry systems to man, and from man back again to invisible gas; of all action, from the imperceptible vibrations of nerve energy to the awful destruction of worlds. All creative potency lies within a Sun sphere. Light is life. The planets are but the offspring of light and life. So in this symbol, we read the source of the human Ego, of our own life. We are, as it were, the planets of the spiritual Sun. Our souls are the attributes of the Sun, of the spiritual Ego. Only from the Ego can we receive life eternal and make immortality a fact. Obeying this spiritual life-force, the human monad is but an attribute, a reflection, of the Divine Ego, and if it fails to awake to a consciousness of this union, it withers and dies like a flower plucked from the parent tree of life.

O child of Adam, in reverence and awe do thou meditate upon this Tablet, for it is a thing of beauty, a being of light, life and love, manifesting its creative mission. It is the Vicegerent of God, flaming forth His splendors in the sky.

TABLET THE SECOND

Mercury

☿

SYMBOL

An elephant, kneeling between two square columns; on one an eagle, on the other a vulture.

At the side a boy, with bow and arrows, standing in doubt which to shoot.

Below these a human face, composed of various flowers, whose roots are snakes, a poppy, forming an eye, which winks.

II

REFLECTION

TABLET THE SECOND

A vision revealing the earthly drama of the microcosm. The elephant represents the highest expression of intelligence, minus the spirit; kneeling between the square columns of matter, i.e., guarded by them. The external mind is sleeping, or, at most, dreaming of the things of the spirit. Above sleeping mind sit the two birds, who represent spirit and matter, each waiting for the slowly preparing feast. The boy, the soul with its weapons, has a choice. Shall it be the sensuality of the flesh that he shall destroy, or the possibilities of the spiritual life on earth. The problem awaits solution. The eagle sits ready to bear aloft the spirit of the sleeper. The vulture hopes for sleep to end in death, that he may live upon the carrion thereof. The flowers of the external mind have for their roots the snakes; and, in a larger sense, the flowers of immortality have the serpent of wisdom for their roots. And the poppy winks. It knows its own power of illusion, and the double significance of the snake; the necessity of evil in the evolution of good. It is the Tablet of Wisdom.

O child of Adam! "Be ye therefore wise as serpents and harmless as doves."

TABLET THE THIRD

Venus

♀

SYMBOL

An altar; on it two cups, one full, the other spilled; near them two bleeding hearts, in one a snake, in the other a dagger.

Above—-clouds, from which comes a woman's face, a wreath in the hand, coming out of the cloud; in the wreath an angel, going upwards, with wings outspread.

III

REFLECTION

TABLET THE THIRD

There is but one altar, but one blood of the sacrament in two cups, but one flesh of the Christ—the Ego—in two hearts, two experiences in love, ecstacy, and pain; two results of experience, the serpent and the dagger, symbolizing wisdom and affliction. Above the altar the divine woman holds the wreath encircling the angel. The angel of immortal life rises from the altar of sacrifice. Some of the wine is spilled as offering. The cup that is filled is raised to "Ra." To serve at the altar of love is the soul-mission of all, even as Christ served his disciples. Each soul must find its own service, and then the pilgrims of the Sun return to the mansions of the blessed. The great mother-god, Venus, Urania, quivers and thrills as she holds forth her offspring—the angel, the young Eros of life eternal.

O child of Adam, this is the Tablet of Love. Meditate thereon, as the last of the triune God. In this Tablet lies the secret of suffering and pleasure. He who vibrates in pain will quiver in ecstacy. Only those who have agonized in Hell can thrill in Heaven.

PART II

———

Here beginneth Chapter 2 of the Second Part of the Book which is
called "The Tablets of Æth," wherein is transcribed the Second
Trinity of the Planetary Rulers.

———

"Thou art called forth to this fair sacrifice
For a draught of milk; with the Maruts
Come hither, O Agni!

They who know the great sky, the Visve
Devas without guile; with those Maruts
Come hither, O Agni!

They who are brilliant, of awful shape,
Powerful, and devourers of foes; with the
Maruts come hither, O Agni!

They who in heaven are enthroned as gods,
In the light of the firmament; with the Maruts
Come hither, O Agni!"

———

"Let us meditate on the adorable light of the Divine Rulers.
May it guide our intellects."

TABLET THE FOURTH

The Moon

> ）
>
> ## SYMBOL
>
> ---
>
> **NIGHT**
>
> A wonderful spider's-web;
> The web glitters in the faint
> moonlight against a dark back-
> ground of blue; moon invisible;
> on the outside of web a star, in
> the center a spot of light, under-
> neath a coffin filled with stones.
>
> ## IV

REFLECTION

TABLET THE FOURTH

The web of life has caught the monad of the soul and thus incarnated the universe, for each soul incarnates its universe at birth, each one's world being different, and peculiar unto himself. At the first breath, the young child polarizes his relations to stars and earth, and it is the affinity and repulsion which make his life experience. And the stars weave the web in their lines of sextile, square and trine, of opposition and conjunction, thus enveloping the monad in the Circle of Necessity.

Outside the star of the spirit, the Ego, shines clear, free from the entanglements of the web and unaffected by the magnetic glamour of the Moon. And lo! the coffin is filled with stones, a symbol of death and the Moon, which is but a casket of stones. Therefore, little monad, caught in the tangle of the web of life and the glamour of earthly things, take heart, for, beyond all, is the star of your being. Call down the law of that star into yourself, and the web is broken and waves its tattered shreds in the breeze. The moonlight, the reflected light, pales as the Star-Sun of your being rises, and the moonlight of Earth gives place to the Sun-spheres of Ra.

O child of Adam! The beginning of sorrow is the dawn of spiritual life. The wise man rules the stars; the fools of Earth obey.

TABLET THE FIFTH

Mars

♂

SYMBOL

———

An immense helmet on
pedestal, across which a streak
of lightning flashes;
beside it a naked child painting
pictures on the helmet;
beneath, a broken sword.

V

REFLECTION

TABLET THE FIFTH

Can greater irony be shown than in this astral symbol. Mars is externally represented as a fierce warrior, awful to behold; the reality, a little child, painting toy pictures on the helmet, too big for his curly head. The lesson in this is indeed, that the pen is mightier than the sword; that the big and blustering helmet will become a plaything for the child. Soon, that the sword of bloodshed, rape, and ruin, will be broken and war relegated to the past, looked at, but, as pictures, painted with hideous reality by the childhood of the race.

The symbol also reveals the great executive forces of humanity, the child. The soul can paint, execute its ideas, its hopes and its fears in any color—the lurid red of blood, the black of ignorance and crime, or in the living light of beauty. All the same, it is the childhood of man painting its ideals in the material world.

O child of Adam, curb the anger of Mars, that thy painting may set the dove at liberty. Let the magic of thy soul transform the savage of the desert into the angel of mercy.

TABLET THE SIXTH

Jupiter

♃

SYMBOL

A cave in the mountain side;
a face like the sphinx comes out
of the cave; there is a blackness
behind it; it looks with upturned
head to a light that is way beyond; it is a face that means
something awful, a godlike defiance to the things that are.

VI

REFLECTION

TABLET THE SIXTH

Again we are impressed with the contrast of internal and external things. Jupiter, the symbol of authority, conservatism, church, and state, and the stability of human institutions, and the things that are, as the things that are the best. But oh, how widely different the internal, the real Jupiter, that governing power of the spirit that hurls defiance at unjust authority, the cruelty and tyranny of the world. The soul sees the light beyond, and, emerging from the dark chasm of matter, knows the battle that must be fought against wrong. It is the awful—yea, terrible—symbol of defiance to gods and men who oppose its onward, upward march to the shining goal of light. Make way, then! Make way! For Earth has given birth to her giant son—the Spirit. For, listen closely, my friend, to the axiom of Immortality. What is soul? Not the spirit, mind you; not the deathless Ego, of which you at present, perchance, know absolutely nothing. Soul is mere memory; a scavenger in earthly states; and a gleaner, a hired help, in the fields of heaven; and to become immortal, there must be something more than soul as the result. It must take such a vital interest in its Lord's work that, finally it becomes too valuable to lose, and must be taken into partnership, so to say. The Ego—Lord— has found a valued servant, a trusted steward, after much seeking, and at once adopts it as its very own. And so the soul becomes heir to the heavenly estate and receives the immortal, vital principle of spiritual union, and awakes from the son of Earth a God-like being, free from the shackles of Time—a dweller in eternity. The soul must awake and realize the Deific atom around which it revolves before it is too late. Unless this is so, the seed of immortal life, sown in matter by the Ego, has not germinated, and it returns unfruitful and dies—it is an abortion. Many, many seeds never germinate. Many good orthodox, but animal-like lives, live, move, and die,—yes, die in very truth. Would to God I could make all mankind realize this awful, inconceivable privilege of life, that, Jupiter-like, they would turn and face the light.

O child of Adam! "It is easier for a camel to go through the eye of a needle than for a rich man to enter into the Kingdom of God."

PART II

Here beginneth Chapter 3 of the Second Part ´ of the Book which is called "The Tablets of Æth," wherein the Third, and last, Trinity of the Planetary Rulers is faithfully transcribed.

"Thou hast entered the immeasurable regions. I am the Dweller of the Threshold. What wouldst thou with me? ° ° ° Dost thou fear me? Am I not thy beloved? Is it not for me that thou hast rendered up the delights of thy race? Wouldst thou be wise? Mine is the wisdom of the countless ages. Kiss me, my mortal lover."

"Thus man pursues his weary calling,
And wrings the hard life from the sky,
While happiness unseen is falling
Down from God's bosom silently."

TABLET THE SEVENTH

Saturn

♄

SYMBOL

———

A human figure with a

scepter of power,

a being of light crowned

with flames.

VII

REFLECTION

TABLET THE SEVENTH

In the external we remember Saturn as an old man, and as a skeleton with a scythe—as Time, in fact. But see, O immortal soul, the real Saturn, as the Angel of Life, having from time gathered the experiences which crown him with light, holding the rod of power; the Christ born in the manger of Capricorn, the Goat—life born of death; the conqueror of evil. He throws off the mask of age, and divine youth beams on us. He doffs the mantle of rags, and royal splendors clothe him. He lifts the hood, and behold the crown. He raises the crutch, and lo! the rod of power. He drops the scythe of death for the jewel of eternal life.

"Om Mani Padme Um."
(Oh the jewel in the lotus.)

O child of Adam! Meditate on the transmutations of life. Behold the earthly miracle of the caterpillar and the butterfly, of the toiling mortal and the transcendent God!

TABLET THE EIGHTH

Uranus

⛢

SYMBOL

———

A human eye,

from which

darts lightning

upon

an ocean of matter.

VIII

REFLECTION

TABLET THE EIGHTH

The state of soul and spirit—penetration; the wonderful power of soul-perception, which sheds its light on all visible things, receiving their images and interpreting them into the spirit, the all-seer—what does it not convey? The perception that can see deep into your soul and see, as it were, the yet unborn thought; that can distinguish the motive of action; that judges the realities of your soul. Such is the Astral Uranian. For with us all, are three planes of mind: The drift plane, the intellectual, and the spiritual, or internal plane; and thought-reading can be on one or all of these different states. But only the Uranian seer can read the inmost mind, and so really know the possibilities of your spirit.

Imagine an image of soft wax, covered with a sensitive skin. All impressions on the skin shape the plastic wax, but go no deeper—do not reach the soul. You can separate these impressions from your real self, when calm and alone, and look upon emotion as a surface play. But the tragedies of life strike deep. They affect the soul, and go to the center of being. *"Verbum sap."*

O child of Adam! Watch the tempest of life closely. The Ego may sit calm amidst the storm, but, if that be stirred—*beware!* The God acts; the soul alone watches.

TABLET THE NINTH

Neptune

♆

SYMBOL

———

A

Winged

Globe.

IX

REFLECTION

TABLET THE NINTH

An unknown quantity, a hope of progression, ideal love, and all true mental and spiritual ideals; aspiration to become that which we feel to be noble and true; the symbol of the monad, the soul which, receiving its life from the Sun—the Ego—is constantly revealing new forces and potencies of that God-life. Each soul's Ego is its maker and God. The Ego is like the Deific potency of the universe, unlimited in potential power, but limited by its monad as to what will be evolved from its awful depth of being. Deity progresses through its expressions of the cosmos. The Ego, your God, finds progressive expression through you, through your soul. That soul is not immortal that becomes separated from its Ego—its God. So, soul, spread your spiritual wings and soar upward.

O child of Adam! Know these three things: Eternity is the creator of the universal life; universal life creates the world, and the world is the creator of time. And of these, the Universe is Life, and the World is Mind, and Time is the Soul. The sum total of all is Experience. And this is individual, conscious life—"*Jacta est alea*" (the die is cast)—the wings are spread.

TABLET THE TENTH

The Cypher — the unknown

O

SYMBOL

———

A Shining Nebulae;

within it a dot,

aimlessly wandering

around an unknown

center.

X

REFLECTION

TABLET THE TENTH

The unknown in very truth. It is everything—it is also nothing. Inconceivable visions arise within the mental universe, but nothing assumes definite form. It is all that is past. It is likewise everything that the future has in store. Amen.

O child of Adam! "Canst thou bring forth Mazzaroth in his season? or loose the bands of Orion?"

CHAPTER XII

PART III

of The Book which is called

THE TABLETS OF ÆTH

———————

OF THE

TEN GREAT KABBALISTICAL POWERS

or

ANGELS OF THE UNIVERSE

PART III

VISION

Each angel standing in front of the symbol is dimly outlined and transparent. Through the angel's form is seen its symbol.

FIRST

A luminous something, which gives the impression of sleep.

SECOND

Something moving, like an ocean.

THIRD

A storm, and lightning.

FOURTH

A mist.

FIFTH

An animal moving, resembling a turtle.

SIXTH

A blue light; in the center a star with three points.

SEVENTH

An expanse of water, a blue sky, a shining disk rising on the horizon.

EIGHTH

A lurid sky, like a red dawn; in the water floats an egg.

NINTH

Five stars on a convex arc, like a rainbow; the shell of the egg is broken and forms continents.

TENTH

A man lying fast asleep under a magnificent palm tree, with his face turned toward the horizon of the sea.

EXPLANATION

Only the pure in heart can see God, and to those pure souls I commend the following brief explanation of the Vision of the Angels of Life, which I have here recorded for the benefit of all whom it may now and hereafter concern.

In the original Vision of the Tablets of Æth a great circle was seen, in the center a head, a faint shimmer above the head, as if the light were about to dawn; a dull, lurid glow beneath, as if of chaos or hell; the hair around the head like floating clouds, the beard like strange cloud-streaks. Each sign of the Zodiac surrounding the center head had within it a faintly seen face. Beginning with the first, it became more and more distinct and perfect with each sign until it evolved into godlike beauty in Pisces.

The symbolic planets were around the Zodiac, and beyond these, making a third grand circle, were the ten Evolutionary Angels. The vision is that of the evolution of all life, spiritual and material. We gaze at the cosmic sex mystery, and the discerning mind, the loving spirit, can read the correspondence of the great sacred conjugal act of both man and God; of its heights, of its depths, and of all that lies between.

To aid in meditation on the head at the center, herein is written a vision, an experience of the soul in the Sleep of Sialam.

The Hermetic brethren encircled my astral body, which was deeply entranced. *"From whence,"* the great question, quivered through my inmost being. To answer that awful problem of the soul the released spirit went on its fearsome journey, back through star systems; back, back beyond all stars, back to the blackness of nothing—that awful nothing, whose outside ring vibrated with fearful flames; the fiery cherubim, winged, taking all possible shapes, and unformed living shapes. A human flamed and changed and vanished. The tornado of whirling, flashing, chaotic life swirled and drove through the darkness of chaos of nothing from nothing—and that great, unknown abyss *is God!* But the life is *evolutionary*.

Deity is progressive, so never can man cease to be. Never can he return to that awful center of nothingness, or be absorbed within the bosom of the unmanifested being. On, and on, and on, with Deific power, God moves in ever-increasing whirls of evolution.

Thus came the answer of the ages: "From primeval force, from the mighty breath of unmanifested being, through every phase of action and reaction, from the energies of storm and lightning, from star-dust to sunlight, has come the spirit of man!"

And the Astral Brethren understood.

THE TWO SEALS OF THE EARTH

I

SYMBOL

———

A human being, with a
flaming, burning
heart.

II

SYMBOL

———

A round disk inside a light,
as from a sun, conceived,
but not seen.

So here endeth the Book which is called "The Tablets of Æth," transcribed
from the astral originals in the Year of Doom MDCCCXCIII.

"Omnia Vincit Veritas."

"THY KINGDOM COME."

*Very Truly
T. H. Burgoyne.*

(Zanoni)

April, 1893

CHAPTER XIII

PENETRALIA

THE SECRET OF THE SOUL

We have now arrived at our final study, which we have approached step by step amid the labyrinth of the mysteries concealed beneath the Veil of Isis. We stand at last upon the very threshold of the sacred Adytum, the "Holy of Holies," from whence proceeds our final revelation of that inmost conception of Man's identity with his Creator—the Penetralia of his Being—the last secret of the incarnated soul.

The written word almost fails us—does fail in fact, when we come to the difficult task of externalizing ideas, the sublimity of which is so infinitely beyond the crystallized images of matter that, they can only be realized in their true glory, when the purified soul can view them from the ineffable heights of eternal spirit. We are lost, dazed, at the brilliancy of the spiritual imagery that opens out before us, in its fathomless stretch of the eternities that are past, of the ever-imperishable present, and the unborn eternities yet to be; all of them linked together in one grand chain of spiritual relationship and deathless identity; as Man, the Angel, God; and God, the Angel, Man; as the triune Cycle of Being, within the incomprehensible Cycle of Necessity; which constitutes Nature's cosmic university for the complete graduation, education, and purification, of that self-conscious, Deific atom of life, whose expression becomes the human soul. Ah! my brothers could you, but for one single instant, realize *who* you are, *where* you are journeying, and *what* your final destiny, every earthly moment at your disposal would be rightly used, and every hour considered too short for your efforts to aid your fellow-man. Selfishness, wealth, and power, would be so utterly contemptible in your sight that their possession would be considered a fearful affliction and a curse, the moment they exceeded the comfortable requirements of mundane existence.

Leave self and the world behind you for the present, and, for the moment, leave your life, with its manifold vanities, in the outer court, and together let us cross the threshold and enter the door of the Temple. There! At last we have entered the Sacred Sanctuary, my brother, and we stand face to face with the imperishable truth of our being—the truth which makes us free, the truth which must ultimately prevail, by virtue of its own inherent Divinity; and we realize Man as he really is, not as he outwardly seems to be. We view him as a molecule, composed of a congregation of separate atoms, all of them held in their places by the centripetal force of the central human atom of life. And yet, small as he is, small as his kingdom is, compared with the mighty creation of which he is a part, he possesses all the inherent qualities of the whole. This, then, is our first conception—Man, is a microcosmic molecule, an atom of divine life.

The scene changes within the chamber, and upon the shimmering, luminous veil, yet before us, we view the large and mighty planet called the Earth. Not as a revolving satellite of the Sun, but as she really is, a vital organ of the macrocosm, the stellar womb of the solar system, the matrix which produces the material organic form of humanity. When "the Earth was without form and void," as we are informed in the mystical language of Genesis, the human soul had not yet reached the state, or grade, in the celestial university that desired the Earth and its temporary illusions. Hence this state was void, an unborn idea, the To Be, and darkness, symbolical of complete lack of life and intelligence, "was upon the face of the deep," silent space.

Again the scene changes, and one by one the numberless planets, planetoids, moons, meteors, comets, and other attendant bodies, pass before the eye of the soul as we gaze upon the curtain of this Sacred Penetralia, each orb belonging to some portion of the Astral Man, each great planet constituting some vital function of the macrocosmic organism, and conferring those qualities upon each and every single atom pertaining to that degree of life, so that the solar system becomes individualized as a grand cosmic organism, its attendant satellites constituting its vital organs, and the shining Zodiac its outward form. So, also, each planet is a living, cosmic individual, intensely alive; living, moving, breathing, and bringing forth its offspring of like substance, matter, in obedience to the potential demand of incarnating spirit. The Sun is alive, glowing with life, and constitutes the heart and arterial center of all the circulating fluids of the stellar anatomy.

Scientists may continue to predict, as they have been predicting, the day when solar radiation will cease, but their predictions will prove as worthless as the sighing of the summer wind, so far as reality is concerned. "It is an incomprehensible mystery to science," says Sir Robert Ball, in his "Story of the Heavens," "how the Sun has been able to maintain its heat with such regularity in the past, for there has been no appreciable change in the Earth's temperature for thousands of years." What it is to-day it was ten thousand years ago—yea, Sir Robert Ball, and will be in ten thousand years to come. You may wonder, and the Royal College may wonder, but in the meantime the mighty, pulsating Sun continues beating out its rhythmic vibrations of spiritual and dynamic life—continues, and will continue, to send the exhilarating current throughout every atom, to the remotest part of his solar dominions, and the same current *returns to him again, undiminished,* for the purification which his glowing, transmuting photosphere alone, can give, to be sent forward again, upon its mission of light, life, and love, around the vital, organic worlds of the astral organism. There is nothing lost, no radiation of energy dispersed upon the unformed, lifeless ether. From the radiating solar focus of Divinity it comes, and to him, undiminished it returns, and so on forever and ever; until the last Deific atom has won its laggard way back to the shining throne of God.

The Sun breathes. The pulsating process of dynamic respiration, eternally repeated during the grand period of a solar lifetime, renews its vital energies, and supplies itself, with the full abundance of the ever-living spirit, transmitted from the shoreless ether in which it lives. It needs no other food, except the magnetic nutriment it receives from each vital organ, or planet, in return for the electrical life current it transmits to them. Just as the human lungs inflate themselves with the vital atmosphere, (which is only the ether, dynamically diluted by the Earth to harmonize with our conditions), to oxygenate the blood and add fresh fuel to the physical furnace, or supply finer essences to the nervous centers. Just as the human heart, with its continual, rhythmic pulsations, propels forth the circulating fluid to every part of the human frame; so does the central heart and lungs of the Grander Man of the Skies, (the Sun) send forth its vitalizing energy to every part of the universe.

Such are the crowding thoughts, born of interior knowledge, that flood the mind as we view these sacred revelations within the sacred chamber of the soul. As yet, we are gazing upon the undulating flow of the astral light. We yearn within our utmost being to become the center of the Penetralia and gaze upon the glorious radiance of the Adonai, from whose ineffable presence we are only screened by the last shining veil of semi-transparent matter, that waves and trembles with every spiritual aspiration. The soul sends forth its pleading cry for light: "Who and what is God?" Faintly, as the distant vesper sounds upon the cooling eve, comes the answer: "Who and what art thou? What canst thou see? What delectable blessing does Nature vouchsafe to the pure in heart?" We tremble with the awful, yet thrilling, revelation. We know dimly, yet fail to realize in our outward consciousness the full import thereof. We realize wherein the mistaken selfhood hath become the only begotten of the Father, but the revelation is too much, and too little. We know that, faint as the voice seemed to the yet unprepared soul, an echo only, *it was the voice of the Adonai behind the veil.* And now we crave the knowledge of the Where and Whither.

Again, we see the Earth as the vital function of the interplanetary being. It is composed of substance termed matter, which substance is the aggregation of countless atoms, which science has not, and never can, resolve into their individual selves. These atoms are rings of the atomless ether, which, thus differentiated from the formless ether, become centers of force, the center of such force being a vacuum within the atomic ring—a center so small that a microscope with lens one thousand times as powerful as the most perfect modern instrument would fail to reveal it. These atoms form systems, under the control of another apparent vacuum; or, rather, this vacuum seems to be the focus, or center, about which they revolve. *This system constitutes a scientific molecule of matter,* and, in response to the innumerable vibrations, they assume different forms or dimensions, and become, indifferently, molecules of oxygen, hydrogen, nitrogen, or carbon, as the case may be, all of which are but different modes of motion of the same primitive atoms, there being in Nature but three things—Ether, Intelligence, and Motion. What Ether is, no one knows. We call it the formless spirit, the unmanifest, etc. But, there can be no doubt but, that Motion is the product of Intelligence, since we never see Motion but as the manifestation of evolution, and this is the expression of Mind. Therefore, we have a duality—Ether and Intelligence; one the living spirit, the other the eternal substance for its manifestation.

Every molecule of matter is the outward form, the center of which, is the incarnating spirit, in some degree of progress. Man's physical organism is a system of life and development for countless billions of them. So the Earth, in its functional expression as the womb of Nature for the outward expression of Man, is only so in a material sense. *He is prior to the planet.* He (Man) is only the off-spring of the planet by virtue of his material body being a part of the substance of the Earth. This life is a stage, only, of his material journey; and, just as Man's body is continually throwing off useless dead matter and replacing the same with new life, so, too, the count-less organic forms of Earth are hourly returning to the ground from which they sprang, and new forms, rising from the same dust, are taking their places.

Here, then, is the sum total: First is revealed to us the grand Astral Man, the Zodiac being the outward idea or form, the Sun and his system the vital functions thereof. The Earth, apart from its functional expression or place, is also an individual. Man, apart from forming a molecule of the planetary womb, by comparison, is also an individual. And, lastly, every molecule of Man's organism is also, in reality, an individual, and small only by comparison with the human frame. And as there are the high Solar Archangels of the Sun, and a chief amongst these seated upon his throne of fire, so there is an Archangelic Chief of the Earth, surrounded by descending degrees of wisdom and power to Man, who also, in his turn, stands as the Deific center and chief of his being, his soul being the sphere of conscious-ness, which, when united to the feminine soul, constitutes the Angel of Life, Eternal. Down still we go, and find that this Divine scale of life and being is, from the lowly molecule, system upon system climb-ing, sphere upon sphere, upward and onward, forever, evermore, and all eternity cannot bring nearer the end of Man's glorious immortality.

In the full revelation of this divine scheme of creation, so full of light, life, love, joy and harmony, a scheme void of death and annihila-tion, the mind once more reflects upon the physical illusions of slowly advancing scientific thought. Camille Flammarion, the great psycho-materialist of France, has painted, in his various novels, a lurid, almost horrible, picture of what the mighty universe must become from the

logical deductions of his own school of thought; a school which would
be best named as transcendental materialism. According to this conception, "thousands, aye, millions of worlds are rushing through space,
inert, frozen, and dead. Suns have cooled down and ceased to give
forth the life-sustaining element of light, but have still retained their
mighty attraction upon their attendant planets, according to the laws
of gravity, by virtue of their material mass, and thus hold their planetary offspring in the eternal, cold, icy grasp of death. Our Sun,
too, is cooling fast; the Earth has already lost a great portion of her
own internal heat. She has passed her prime of life, and death—cold,
icy death—has already begun to encroach upon her extremities. The
South pole (the feet) is now practically lifeless in one perpetual
covering of ice. So, too, her head; her locks are the white of perpetual
snow. No longer has she the blush and beauty of youth, no longer
adorned with the healthy covering of verdue which youthfulness gives,
and as our geologists prove was once the case. So that, although the
time may still be long, according to our reckoning of years, it is only
a brief moment in eternity when this fair Earth, and also the beauteous
splendor of the silent stars, will be locked forever in darkness, and
the final sleep of doom." If this be so, we ask of the inmost soul, if
life be but the fitful awakenings of the indestructible spirit, ebbing
and flowing in response to the rise and fall of Nature's cosmic ba-
rometer and the transmutations of matter; if life is, in reality, but a
brief and passing moment, eternally repeated, from the flush of youth,
"the gilded salon to the bier and the shroud, then why, O why should
the spirit of mortal be proud?" Why aspire to penetrate the inward
realities of life and enter the Holy of Holies—to seek and find out
God? As the rushing torrent of this thought swept o'er the mental
chambers of the soul and saturated the spirit with its icy sting, as it
lay still chained within the prison house of matter, the higher self rose,
sublime in its grandeur, and consciousness of divine relationship, and,
in the last earthly appeal for light, for divine truth, as to Man and
his immortality, it turned in reverence and awe before the still, shimmering veil of the sacred Penetralia. The trial had come, the crucial
test, whether of life or death, the final revelation to Man. In purity of
heart and humility of soul we await in agonizing suspense. There is a
thrilling sensation, as though of ten thousand electric currents consuming the frame, and a swaying to and fro, as if drifting upon an

ocean of fire; then a dead silence, so profound that whole eternities seem to pass, without either beginning or end. And the sight of the inward spirit is opened slowly. Who? Where? What? For the shadows have fled, the luminous curtain fades, is gone, and flashing before the inward sight stands the ineffable Adonai. It is I—you! There is no God but this, and in one moment the interior consciousness becomes at-one-with-self, God, and from that inconceivable height of profound vision we again look upon Nature. Behold Sun, Moon and planets in all the original magnificence of their nebulous luminosity; from nebulous rings we proceed, stage after stage, each producing its own degrees of life. On, on we pass the ages, the geological cycles of inconceivable duration in time, but only a mere instant in eternity; and on and on, as the changes roll, until we see Earth as she is now; still on, at the ever-urging desire of the triumphant Soul, and a remarkable change is apparent. From forces, at present latent, there comes a change; and, instead of so-called physical; electrical races have superceded the present humanity. Crystallization has ceased; and all things become lighter in density and more ethereal in nature; *and the orbit of the Earth grows less.* Nearer and nearer shines the mighty Sun; first Vulcan, then the swift messenger of the gods are indrawn within the solar vortex, each absorption producing a cataclysmic change upon our Earth. Then comes the turn of Venus, while slowly and surely the orbit of the Earth contracts, and nearer shines the Sun. And, finally, the beautiful Earth, her mission over, the last atom of life beyond her rule, inward she sweeps, and is lost in the mighty ocean of fire as a stone is lost in the lake. Verily is the word of prophecy a literal truth: "The Earth shall be destroyed with fire." And so on with the rest, each planet in its proper turn fulfilling the functions at present performed by the Earth, each becoming the grand theater of material and ethereal life, and the cometary bodies, to-day chasing unknown orbits in the realms of ether, gradually fall into line when their erratic cycle is ended, taking the places of the present outermost planets.

No such thing as death, no such thing as the dark silence of eternal night, for any organic creation of the Most High. From the Sun they come, and unto the Sun each must ultimately return, even as the body of Man, coming from the dust of Earth, must also return thereto, to be taken up in new forms and furnish substance for other degrees of life. And thus will it be, until the Sun, in its mighty solar heavens of purified spiritual life, will form the last, the final battle ground of matter, receiving *its new life from a greater center than itself*. A glorious solar world, well typified in the last Battle of the Gods, and the new Earth—a World whereon the Angels tread in superlatively beautiful forms, clothed with the ideals and emanations of their own divine purity—Souls clothed in Air, treading the ethereal Realms of Light, as the children of God, and the inheritors of the Kingdom of Heaven.

Must the searching eye of the Soul seek further? Must the insatiable thirst of the Spirit launch out upon the trackless infinities of the yet To Be? Must it still penetrate further in the profound beyond, where time ceases to be, where the past, present, and the future, are forever unknown, but exist only as the Deific consciousness of the eternal Now? No. The Soul at last rests satisfied. The final revelation is over.

My brother, we have done; and, in closing, have only to add that, not until the speculating philosophy of earthly schools blends with the Science of the Spheres in the full and perfect fruition of the wisdom of the ages, will Man *know* and *reverence* his Creator, and, in the silent Penetralia of his inmost being, respond, in unison with that Angelic Anthem of Life: "We Praise Thee, O God!"

FINIS of the first edition.

CHAPTER XIV

QUOTATIONS FROM LESSONS

Quotations and answers from private lessons of Hermetic Teachers. These are in addition to those given in Chapter V, Vol. I, of The Light of Egypt.

You cannot receive much knowledge from the reading of books. You must learn to contact the subjective currents of thought and wisdom by developing the intuitional and spiritual nature, and by the daily practice of psychomitry, meditation on high spiritual subjects and aspirational breathing with an earnest desire for the true knowledge of Nature's occult truths; thus you can contact or call down knowledge.

In Dynamic Breathing by Genevieve Stebbins, aspirational breathing is described as follows;—

1. Stand upright in a normal position.

2. The hands being at the sides, raise them slowly so as to describe a circle, meeting like a spire above the head.

3. While the hands are slowly undergoing this evolution, inhale while you count seven beats.

4. Hold the hands and breathe in position while you count three beats.

5. Exhale the breath while you count seven beats, bringing the hands slowly down in unison, pressed together in front of the face in the form of prayer, continuing the motion until they part company at the abdomen.

6. Keep the lungs empty during three beats, and then continue this exercise.

The mental idea for this exercise is that aspiring for Divine illumination and power, which exalts the whole being. The imagination responds by feeling the spiritual influx of joyous inspiration.

No matter what we know we have no right to deprive anyone of their chance or privilege of trying. Each person should be allowed to make their own choice and thus strengthen their own character and learn from experience.

After the death of its physical body, a soul does not suffer before awakening to consciousness. Cremation of the body frees the soul from matter, then it may awaken more quickly and be free to seek its proper sphere in the soul world through the laws of affinity and merit. Its true desires, shown by its life while on earth, determines the soul sphere where it begins. We begin there where we leave off here and must correct all former errors before we can advance.

When a soul is forced from its physical body by obsession, the soul suffering is caused by its regrets in not being able to remain the occupant and ruler of its own tenement, conditions and causes of the change increase or decrease the suffering.

The spiritual birth of a person while yet in the physical body is not any sudden change in the body. The change takes place slowly. When the mental and soul qualities have become so refined through sincere desire and earnest study that they can vibrate to much higher conditions they are gradually raised to a higher plane of vibration and this consciousness is slowly impressed upon the physical brain.

The soul is always conscious and knows interiorly, inwardly, the truths and realities of Nature. And to be soul conscious we must realize externally the realities of the soul's knowledge. And to accomplish and bring this about we must sensitize and polish our brain or plate so these truths can be reflected perfectly, externalized. Then, and then only, are we soul conscious. Unkind thoughts, false thoughts, criticism, hasty judgments, fault finding, etc., etc., so blur our mirror and fog our brain, that the reflections from the Soul world (the world of realities) become distorted, out of shape, become error and thus constitute non-realities to us.

I reason from the law of correspondences, that, upon the physical plane, the man or positive nature seeks woman or the negative nature. So per contra. Upon the Soul plane the feminine soul is the positive and the masculine soul the negative, consequently the soul of woman must seek for its true mate, the soul of man. The law is LOVE. She must, through intense but calm soul love draw to her, her counterpart or soul mate. After having once met, whether consciously or not, they forever after vibrate in unison, each filling up the deficiencies in each other. Man desiring this union must not be too positive or else he will repel and defer the meeting. The physical meet upon the personal plane, the mental or intellectual upon the plane of individuality and the Souls upon the plane of identity to become as one, the Spiritual Ego.

When the power of imparting joy is equal to the will, the human soul requires no other heaven.   Queen Mab.

The Solar Plexus is the center of contact for occult forces because we are a septenary being;—a physical trinity, a soul trinity, and the divine ego (the 7th. or whole). The Solar Plexus is the center of our physical being. From that region, our body drew from the physical mother all the requisites for the complete growth, nutrition and perfect gestation of our body. Therefore, it must be the most delicate and sensitive part of our organization, the most fitting receptacle for the connecting link from the subjective or soul trinity, the occult forces. The center of our subjective being (the Soul) vibrates naturally to the center of our physical being. The spiritual has its center of contact in the crown of the head. The sexual organs are the center of contact for the physical.

Vibration and Polarization. Vibration is an invisible force moving to and fro between two points or poles. These two points may be two objective objects or two subjective states, or one may be objective and the other subjective. These two points of the vibratory motion determine the polarity of that force moving between them. If the vibrations are discordant or inharmonious, the obstacles that lie in the path of this moving force must be removed or one or both points of polarization must be changed. This is accomplished, wholly and solely, by or through the will ability. Therefore, the first thing to do is to cultivate the interior will to a supreme degree and strength. As an illustration;—overcoming any evil tendency is changing the polarity of that evil force we vibrate to, that which feeds and strengthens the evil tendency within us. Or we must desire, think, act and be the exact opposite of any evil in us to change the polarity to good. Truly, "man may be what he wills to be."

Vibration depends upon the density, firmness and sensitiveness of the object vibrated. A rod of iron will produce a dull thud when struck, while a fine, dense, tightly strung wire of a musical instrument when struck by the key will give forth a beautiful, pleasing sound. But a musical instrument requires an operator to produce the vibrations that result in harmonious music. Iron, coal, stone, etc., in their denseness vibrate to the lowest spheres of earth, but in their course of evolution these substances become less dense and more sensitive or refined and the vibrations become finer and more intense. It is so with humankind, the body vibrates to the corresponding atoms of the atmosphere (surrounding conditions), soul and body should vibrate in perfect harmony. Our souls are the musicians and our bodies are the instruments, therefore, we must tune our body by systematic training, care and good attention until it is in perfect tune and under the absolute control of the soul;—then the result will be perfect vibration, perfect time, tune, harmony, allowing us to enjoy the music of the spheres.

Kindle the spark of eternal progress and it can never be quenched, except by the Neophyte's own will. Life is eternal and man can not stop the progress of another, only place a stumbling block in his path. To gain wisdom, keep alive the spiritual fire, by earnest work, study and meditation, using the light you now have and may receive. Action (mental and spiritual) is life, inertia death. Nor should you neglect the body. Make every effort which duty imposes upon you to secure the comforts necessary for health, peace and a quiet mind for study. You will then be making true progress. Of all creatures, MAN alone, has the God given ability to consciously develop his spiritual senses so as to be able to use them in observing the operations of the true laws of life and thus learn the causes of what we experience here on earth.

Demonstrate by your lives the truths we seek to impart and you will attract to yourselves peace. These teachings will give you a greater scope of knowledge than you now dream is possible. Comprehension will be more clear and true; not all the world then can rob you of that interior peace which is the result of unfoldment and true knowledge of self. As the soul advances in the path of esoteric knowledge fears and doubts disappear and a firm and abiding faith take their place.

Monastic life, The rule of Saint I AM;—this subject is a broad one and I am afraid too intricate to be answered in a letter. A volume would do but scant justice to it. There are two diametrically opposite views of monastic life and institutions, both of them absolutely true;—a paradox to be sure but so indeed is everything connected with the human mind. The positive and purely intellectual view is that, all things considered, we know but little of earth and practically nothing of heaven, therefore, the present life is the problem of man. The future can well afford to look after itself, etc. The real hero, it is thought, is he who enters into the bustling life of today, shares its problems, national and individual, in fact, leads an active, assertive, vital life, and if to this he adds honor, virtue and charity, conquers all temptations to wrong doing, and finally makes life a substantial success morally and financially according to the ideal of his generation, such a man is a true hero, an ideal man, an example to follow, and considering the plane of life from which this view is is taken, it is undoubtedly true. This modern hero is a man who lived amongst men, who did his duty according to law, and who fighting a good fight, lived merely, worthily and well, and so far as earthly consideration goes, what more can be desired?

The opposite or spiritually religious view can be summed up in few words;—Earth is nothing; Take no thought of what ye shall eat or what ye shall drink, etc. The world is the playground of Satan, all physical pleasures are snares and entrap the soul. Repentance for uncommitted crime, aspiration and prayer for a peace which seems ever near and which, in fact, never comes. The atonement of Christ and the Nirvana of Buddha, these are the ascetic ideas of monks and Sama alike. All the rest of earth becomes to them a curse, a temptation and a snare. The world with its wine, women and song is a corruption of the flesh and the devil. In fact all manifested nature, with its love, life and power is but vanity and vexation of spirit. And even this side from the plane of the spiritual ideal is true. The two views represent the two opposite sides of man's nature, the monk and the merchant. The one seeks honor with real estate on earth;—the other a crown with undisputed titles in heaven. They are both right and they are both equally wrong when life in its one grand aspect is taken into consideration.

Here then is the Hermetic standpoint, the true plane from which all things must ultimately be viewed. Though before going further let me borrow an expression from the old astronomer poet of Persia; *"The worldly hope men set their hearts upon, Turns to ashes or it prospers and anon, Like snow upon the desert's dusty face, Lighting a little hour or two is gone."*

The last line of this quotation contains the real gist of every perfect rule that will apply to man in his biune nature;—man the individual and man the enfranchised soul of divinity on earth or in heaven, within the whirl of worldly life or soaring as a divine thought amid the stars, the same absolute truth becomes manifest. This, now, requires an explanation. To begin with I will present you with a few considerations.

1st. Man was prior to this present life and will be posterior to it.

2nd. Man is the most perfect expression of the divine idea up to date, so far as earth is concerned. He is the climax of evolution.

3rd. Man's nature, broadly speaking, is dual, physical and spiritual, therefore, the interplay brings into being a third factor, the mental, which is neither wholly one nor the other.

4th. Man as a bi-une entity, if he would be progressive, must lead two lives and feed both sides of his nature, otherwise, one side will suffer to the serious detriment of the other. A purely physical or animal life or existence will starve the soul and result in Spiritual death, so to speak. On the contrary a purely spiritual life, such as has been led by some ascetics, destroys the natural functions of the body and by re-action warps the intellectual faculties so that the mind, becoming diseased, cannot discern unbiased truth, no matter how logical such truth may be to others. The mind is warped and distorts every idea to harmonize with its own dominant error, whatever that may be. When the intellectual lens is out of focus angelic revelations become spiritual delirium.

5th. Man as a dual entity, possessing a threefold nature, physical, mental and spiritual, has also the *possibility* of absolute immortality. Man, as man merely, is *not* immortal, and if nothing beyond the animal man is present or sustained when it is present, nothing but the animal will survive death, and that being matter will follow the transformations of matter. But man as a spiritual atom of life is immortal. This spiritual entity should dominate its human envelope, granting to each zone of its life a proper, lawful expression in the body, in the mind and in the soul. Such a course of life is perfect, for it sustains and develops every department of man's being.

6th. The true aim of a perfect life is to follow out the law of evolution which gave it being, which law requires a recognition of every phase of life upon its own plane with an eternal aspiration toward an ideal that evolves and expands in perfect proportion with our upward march through the eternities yet to come, ever beyond, but ever bright and clear. When this is attained, instead of the magnet of our mother earth, we shall follow the shining star of the Magi whose radiant center is the lode-stone of God.

7th. Therefore, it becomes apparent that the *real, true living,* to begin with, consists in taking all things as we find them. Shirk none. With honest, fearless purpose meet all, and by so doing become a center of power and purpose. Make your own environment out of the material at hand. The outward doth from the inward roll, and the inward dwells in the inmost soul.

Having carefully digested the foregoing considerations you will note that my opinion regarding monastic life is that everything depends upon the monk. A man or woman should have a full and complete experience of life and love of pleasure, sorrow and pain; should know what physical pleasure can give and what delights, amidst literature, science and art, the intellectual life has to offer. When this is the case the man or the woman is no longer young, but on the contrary, will be matured in body and mind. Such people are in small danger then of becoming either prejudiced cranks or hallucinated fools. To these and *to these only* monastic life, or the retirement from the material strife of the world will generally prove a great spiritual blessing and profitable to mind and body and soul. It is then to such as these who in addition to a spiritual life wish to get back to Nature and live near to the primitive sources of life, away from the city mart, to the heart of the pines, and there in the "Forest of Arden" resting upon the bosom of the kindly earth breathe with her, indrawing her vital strength and learning therefrom those deep mysteries of being which are the primitive sources of life, religion and art, that I give the simple rule of the ancient Order founded by *Saint I am.*

The Rules of Saint I am

1. Each human body becomes its own monastery, church and temple.

2. Each member of the Order is forever his own Abbot and earthly superior so far as the rules and conduct are concerned.

3. There are two days in each year that every member of the Order shall consider as unworthy of serious concern and these are *yesterday* and *tomorrow*. Yesterday is beyond recall and its only value is that of experience. Sorrowing over the past is childish and mental anxiety over the future is simply idiotic, since we do not live therein. Life is forever the eternal present and all else is vanity and vexation of spirit. The true life will learn to profit by the past because of its lessons of errors; to live nobly in the present because of the *here and now,* the very nick of time in which all things are accomplished; and be optimistic with unbounded hope and faith in the future. But what is said herein about the past must not be understood as indifference. Keen repentance is required of each soul for past sin, but it must be sorrow for the *sin, not a regret for the past,* not a wish to recall it, but a thankfulness in sorrow that we may profit by the error as experience, and never again commit the same fault.

4. Live one day at a time, beginning with the morning meditation as in the rules for training. Assert yourself and be a man or woman. Speak quietly, refrain from hurry, be calm and enjoy the beauties of Nature under whatever aspect they present themselves; for when the Lord God saw everything which He had made, and, behold, He saw that it was very good.

5. Do good to others and no evil for this is the law of life, its violation is death. Give of the fruits of thy knowledge for this is charity. Point out the pathway of eternal life, for this is the essence of hope and faith. But ever remember that a wise gardener will not waste his present time in watering a withered tree, for this will not profit him nor his brethren in this world nor the next.

6. In all things essential be positive and assert your divine right, become the *I AM.* In all things non-essential take the line of least resistance, for it is a criminal waste of energy to fight when the battle is not worth contention. Let it always be understood among the members of this ancient order of beings that in all things essential there must be unity; in non-essentials absolute liberty, and finally in all things, under all circumstances, there must be charity.

7. No one should live in idleness, but each must be the sole judge as to *what is work,* for life in itself depends for its fruits on

motion. It is good, bad or indifferent, according to the point of view and the mental attitude assumed toward it, therefore, members may live singly or in community as best suits their needs or desires and may adopt any number of rules and regulations for their government from time to time, providing that they do not in any way conflict with the rules here given of the *Saint I AM*.

This is, then, the kind and condition of monastic institution which the Hermetic Brothers consider broad and catholic enough to admit every one but fanatics, and safe enough in discipline for every one but fools, and with these two latter the Brothers of *Saint I AM* can have no fellowship.

Hymn XV. of the Book of Wisdom, Vol. I, page 130, reads;—

"Strive by concentrating the thought (mind) to liberate the supreme Soul, pure and free of the envelopes (Elements) to which she is united, that the body and the other, in the same wise as is sifted the grain from the chaff."

The Elements here referred to are the intelligent forces of Nature, generated by the four primary elements of Air, Fire, Earth and Water, or the elementals of the astral planes and attached to *us* as we produce or create the corresponding elementals within our spheres. There are both *good* and *evil* in each of these elemental kingdoms and we create by our thoughts and acts their affinities. To progress we must create the good and overcome and eliminate the evil before the Soul is free to advance. The good are created by acts of kindness, generosity, unselfishness, liberty to all, energy, ambition, desire, aspiration, activity, expression and fearlessness in the cause and promotion of truth, love and charity to all of God's creatures, etc., etc. To avoid the evil and malicious inhabitants of these kingdoms we must not create their affinities by thoughts of hate, envy, fear, revenge, jealousy, malice, selfishness, dishonesty, etc., etc. The elementals of *fire* are known as Salamanders. The elementals of *earth* are known as Gnomes and the *evil* belong wholly to the earth because of their desire of wealth, show, earthly glory and power, cant, drinking, eating, debaucheries, lusts of the flesh, monopolies, etc. Here, the desirable creations are those of *duty*, power and possessions to meet the duties of the hour, those we have assumed and those that are thrust upon us. Desire the comforts for body and mind and the means necessary to accomplish the duties for which we are responsible and the requisites needed to aid in the furtherance of all movements to assist the improvements and uplifting of humanity, etc. The elementals of the *airy* kingdom are the Sylphs and the affinities of this realm are the creations of ideals. So, beware of drawing to yourself the evils created by false illusions, wrong ideas, jealousy, false thinking, unreasonableness, false judgments, insinuations of wrong, defaming, gossip, etc., etc. Create the *good* by clean, pure thoughts, beautiful ideals and ideas, wishing thoughts of kindness, love, good will and charitableness to all humanity, etc. The Undines belong to the *watery* kingdom which is the creative sphere. Therefore, not to bind ourselves to the *evil* elementals and powers of this plane, we must not accept any false creeds or dogmas, no false conceptions of truth, no false christs, no false teachers, leaders or friends. Nor must we create any false conceptions of truth, nothing that cannot be proven by the law of correspondences, "as it is above so it is below; as on the earth so in the sky." Conceive in truth and try to know Nature as taught by this Hermetic rule and live in harmony with the natural laws of life.

Aphorisms for the Great Truths;—by The Hermetic Teachers.

Concerning life and immortality, my soul longs and asks for, as the burning sands of the desert cry out for the rain. In the air I breathe; in the music that comes to my ear; in the beauties of nature that I see; my inmost soul tells me is my God. Give to me the ears of knowledge and understanding to hear with; the eyes of faith and love to see with. Give to me the wisdom to say, I know; I am—that—I am. Time without beginning, time without end.

Inspiration;—that harp divine whose strings the angels tune, and set in motion sweet waves of music, that vibrates around the spheres, that brings to man the tidings of his once celestial state, and says in tones of heavenly sweetness, to faint and struggling souls, "Look ever up and onward, thy spirit calls thee home." God, Jehovah is, and thou must be.

Omnia, Vincit, Veritas.

The light that shines from the pinnacle of truth, can never grow dim; the fogs of ignorance and superstition may obscure, but cannot extinguish. It is your duty and work to aid human improvement, to put forth every effort to dispel that fog and set the bells of good tidings to ringing, peace on earth and good will to all.

Knock, and it will open. (Physical) work.

Ask, and ye shall receive. (Mental) study.

Seek, and ye shall find. (Spiritual) meditate.

Aphorisms;—subjects for deep thought and silent meditation, to aid in spiritual growth and understanding.

1. Learn self poise.

2. Learn the inward calm that can express the outward calm.

3. Interior calmness aids the physical confidence and confidence is necessary upon the physical plane.

4. Learn the decision that comes from the inward knowledge. Never let the seeming to be, nor the wishing it to be so, warp the judgment.

5. Ignorance is weakness, weakness begets doubt, and doubt is the undoing of the soul.

6. Be careful of forming a wrong idea of any person or thing, that you hold in the mind till you make of it a reality; for it will remain with its parent to give doubt, fear, and will deceive the soul until the wrong done has been atoned for.

7. An unconquered strife that is hidden in the soul, is more consuming than a raging fire.

8. Say ye not *nay* about any person, for ye know not the beginning. Say ye not *yea*, because ye know not the why. Say ye not so is so, for only God is absolute.

9. Think not these things at all; for in the thinking ye dwell longest upon them, and therein lies the greatest danger, for the undoing of thy self and for the fogging and numbing of thy spiritual growth.

10. Do and think unto others as you would have them do and think unto you.

11. Give thou unto an evil one the chain for which he asks, and straight way in anger at thy generosity will he hang himself to the end of it.

12. Strive continually for the domination of the spirit over all the actions of your life. Strive to uplift and beautify all the paths where in you have to walk and work. By so doing, you open the door for the inflowing of the spirit.

13. Faith is the avenue to the soul plane, for which interior calmness is required.

14. Persistent determination in the face of all obstacles, is true faith. Faith is strength; by this strength (faith) the soul gains power to mount higher and higher in its search for knowledge, therefore its deliverance.

15. Hope is the calm confidence in faith. Hope is the anchor of the soul. Hope is confidence that one will obtain the object desired.

16. Charity and love make all things possible to the soul, that is earnestly trying to work out its immortal destiny, Love of truth and the things that represent truth. Charity for those that have not found the truth, nor the things that stand for truth, and are working in darkness. Charity, blessed charity, is a balm to the misguided soul; all else of earth is as naught in comparison to it. Wipe away the tears, extend the helping hand, and leave the judging and the judgment to the Most High, thy God.

17. If the water is muddy, you do not clear by stirring; but by the quiet, steady, process of filtering. If the filtering is applied a sufficient length of time, the water will surely become clear. So with the muddy waters of ignorance and misunderstanding, use the filter, truth and patience, and the muddy water will just so surely become clear.

18. The soul will grieve; but do not let it grieve for the mental, nor the physical suffering of those trying to live a conscious life; that bring on themselves the suffering by a proud feeling of superiority. Spirit attainments should not give a feeling of proud superiority, but a feeling of humility, and true inward charity for others; not the feeling, I am better than thou, but the God like love and charity that will search with a strong light to find the smallest mite of good, in another.

19. Blessed are the pure in heart, for they can see God. He that is humble in spirit, will be exalted. He that is proud in spirit, will be laid low. Remember, the soul on the wings of faith, soars to where its aspirations call it; let not the soul, by its aspirations, call down the spirit, but be it ever drawn upward by inspirations.

20. Peace on earth and good will to all, is a dictation of the spirit; unless you can fully feel and express this, your own soul can

never realize the peace that passes all understanding.

21. Cold intellect, with only the reason to help it, has to gain its knowledge through external or material avenues. When the intellect alone dominates a person, it will be difficult for them to grasp the true, interior spiritual meaning; except in so much as it may be possible to put it into external, or material form, that will appeal to the intellect only. The inmost spiritual truths, never have, never can, and never will, appeal to any but those that have the interior spiritual ability to comprehend them. The spiritual truths here meant are those, that cannot be demonstrated upon the material plane, and, where the intellect is the only interpreter.

22. The exterior, or external, may be lighted to any extent to which the owner wishes, and can exert the powers of his intellect and reason to obtain. But, what does he see of his possessions? Only a little of the outside, nothing of his real accumulations of years, that he has gathered up to beautify the interior of his house. Let him put the smallest light on the inside and he will immediately begin to see the forms and outlines of objects, that he could not have had, even, the faintest idea of, with all of his outside light. With his interior light, he can open his windows and let others enjoy with him, or shut his treasures in at will. With his light on the outside he could not enjoy, nor let any one else enjoy. So, light that interior spark; if the intellect and reason are in harmony with the interior, all is well; but if not, then remember, the smallest interior light is as far above the outside light, as the stars, by comparison, are above the earth. This external light had much better be in the minority than trying to outshine the true and real light within.

23. The dew drop that rests on the leaf of the rose at sunrise is as necessary as the down pour of rain. Grasp firmly in the mind the fact, and realize it, that in the mighty scheme of creation, absolutely nothing can be lost. To the interior there is no real meaning to the expression great or small, that is figuratively, not in the literal sense, for in the various rounds and states, the infinitely great becomes the infinitely small, and the infinitely small becomes the infinitely great.

24. Hold the strands of life in the mind by the power of intelligence. With the fingers of the soul unweave the threads and trace them back to the beginning. With the magical power of the will,

through aspiration and inspiration, bind them together again into an unbreakable chain, to carry the spirit into those vistas of the future, that ever bids it to go higher.

25. Ever keep that fair mirror of the soul, called faith, clear and bright; never let a ripple mar its placid surface. The divine truths that you see mirrored in it, are for the hungry soul; to give it light and knowledge to carry it back to its divine Ego, in the realms of infinite light that surround the throne of God.

26. As the memory of the past unrolls, let neither exaltation nor fear take possession of the soul. Strive for that perfect calm and poise that will give the clear sight and understanding, to view picture after picture, as the recording angel turns backward the leaves in the book of life.

27. The soul that seeks its divine centre unmindful of trials, pitfalls and suffering; seeing only the star of its destiny shining afar off; will shine forth resplendent as it nears the goal.

28. Prove all things by the light of intelligence with a firm, calm desire to know the truth without prejudice or bias. When the intuitions of thy soul, after prolonged meditation, flashes her light upon the mind accept the solution, then weigh this with reason, the result will be indisputable.

29. The credulous minds always suffer, they are like the foolish virgins who kept not their lamps (intelligence) trimmed and burning.

30. In the economy of Nature nothing is wasted; from the tiny dew drop. to the building and dissolution of worlds, every atom serves its purpose; when that purpose is fulfilled, there comes a change of polarity only; and the same atoms are again utilized by Nature and Nature's Supreme Intelligence carries on the process forever.

31. Over the material destinies of men the planets rule; pointing out the time to act and the time to refrain, the time to sow and the time to reap. They are monitors, (if men would understand) the active agents of divine intelligence expressing *His Will* through the brilliant scintillating jewels of our skies, the radiant gems of the *Master's Crown.*

32. Woe to those who place a stumbling block in the path of any soul's progress. Always encourage the timid and fearful ones by

word and thought, for often the right word in the right place is a strong staff to the weak.

33. Remember that a knowledge of the law of correspondences is necessary to the correct interpretation of symbols. All manifest Nature is a symbol of the divine idea; the expressions of an idea may be manifold.

34. The sincere unqualified love of truth is the best guide in the path of wisdom.

35. Knowledge without understanding is like a ring of gold in a swine's snout.

36. The man who fills his mind with the written words of others, without proving or understanding in his soul, gains not wisdom, but rather the husks.

37. Wisdom may be likened unto refined gold. It is knowledge refined in the crucible of experience. While understanding makes wisdom one's own.

38. The pearl diver must be properly equipped for his work, else it were a perilous undertaking; just so with the seeker after Nature's divine truths. He should know what he is about.

39. By their fruits ye shall know them, means, ye shall know the manner of a person, that is, the plane of intelligence to which they belong, and not that ye shall sit in judgment to condemn or extol.

40. Only the pure in heart may see God. Yea, not until the soul, purified by trial, sorrow and suffering, and having gained complete mastery of self, then, illumined by the interior light, the soul beholds the Adonia.

41. The pursuit of wisdom from a pure love of truth and knowledge is the only surety of success. The "Pearl of Great Price" ever eludes the selfish, ambitious and vain-glorious.

42. Courage, patience and calm confidence in thyself and thy immortal destiny, will give wings to thy soul, strength to thy spirit and bring realization of thy soul's desire.

43. Heed not thy calumniators, for as they have sown, so shall they reap.

44. Cast thy bread upon the waters. It will return in time to bless or curse the sender. So let thy bread (ideas, thoughts and

ideals) be good, pure and light, that it may return to thee in happy realization of past efforts.

45. The past is like an old garment, worn-out and cast away, it may have been worn with grace or the reverse, but the present only is thine, the future is with the Infinite.

46. The pursuit of knowledge is a more royal road than the pursuit of happiness, because of happiness, no two can experience the same degree, nor would happiness so called to one, be held as such by another. But knowledge is the same to all, being neither delusive, nor fleeting. Joy and sorrow, what are they but the fleeting shadows of a day. But wisdom abideth for all time.

47. The peace that passeth understanding is greatly to be desired. It is calm assurance, confidence, to the soul. The mind reflects it and the way of divine wisdom is as the light of the Sun.

48. Prayer consists not in the spoken word uttered without understanding what true prayer is. No, it is the deep unutterable yearning of the human soul for light, for peace and guidance, that will sooner or later be realized.   Amen.

Finis of Aphorisms by The Hermetic Teachers

Originally, The Pyramid was designed as a perpetual observatory, from which, at any and all times, and in all ages, all the facts governing the movements of this world could be deduced from observation of the celestial bodies.

The Riddle of the Sphinx; it symbolizes the astrological basis of the Egyptian Religion and the growth pattern of life.

The Sphinx has stood for centuries in majestic defiance of all the destructive forces of time and the mind of man to solve its mysteries. It is built of living stones.

It symbolizes the esoteric thought of Ancient Egypt, that the universe and all it contains is pulsating with eternal life, whose source is a central spiritual sun of infinite, unconditioned wisdom, containing all that is or will be. That all are but parts of one stupendous whole whose body Nature is and God the soul. That each atom of eternal life involves from spirit to dense matter, then evolves upward through vegetable, animal and human to its spiritual source. That each human being is a miniature universe which its lord or immortal ego must learn to control before it can acquire a true understanding of life.

The Sphinx has the paws of a lion, the body of a bull and the head of a man. These three units symbolize Osiris (the father), Isis (the mother), and Horus (the son);—the eternal trinity of life. The wings of an Eagle are folded close to the body of the bull to indicate silence.

Now we must show how this astrological symbolism can be interpreted to give this hidden meaning.

Osiris (the father), symbolized by the paws of the lion, represents the Solar Lion of the Mysteries, whose constellation is Leo. Leo is the second emanation of the Fiery triplicity and is the constellation of the Sun. This symbolizes GOD, infinite wisdom, the spiritual Sun, the source of eternal life. The Sun passes through the sign Leo in the summer, in July and August, the hottest time of the year.

Isis (the mother), symbolized by the body of a Bull, represents Apis, the Sacred Bull of the Egyptians, whose constellation is Taurus. Taurus is the highest emanation of the Earthy triplicity and is the constellation of the planet Venus. This symbolizes the Universal Mother, the source of all manifestation. God's thoughts put into form. The Sun passes through the sign Taurus in the spring of each year, in April and May, when the forces of life are striving to make all things grow.

Horus (the son), symbolized by the head of a Man, represents the Works Done (all manifestations of God, man being considered the highest and containing in essence all forms of life below himself). Aquarius is the constellation of the archetypal man, and is the lowest emanation of the Airy triplicity and the constellation of the planet Uranus.

The Wings of an Eagle, folded close to the powerful body of the Sphinx, indicate that these intellectual forces work in silence, free of all material matter.

Thus we have the eternal trinity of life in its highest sense. God, infinite wisdom (Spiritual Fire, the essence of life) is the source of all. The spiritual seeds (God's thoughts) are planted in Earth (substance), developed in Water (moisture) and evolved into the Air (atmosphere, space). And all of this is done in silence, is going on continually, before our very eyes, yet how little we understand, truly, mankind are the most ignorant of that which is, life itself.

And again the same thought expressed in a different way.

God, the Spiritual Sun (the Solar Lion, infinite wisdom, life, vital eternal energy) whose constellation is Leo, the second emanation of the Fiery triplicity, plants his spiritual seeds (Immortal Egos) in Earth or substance, where they can grow or manifest on each of the three planes of life, Spiritual, Mental (Astral), and Physical (Material).

The Sacred Bull, Taurus (Mother Nature, the slow, patient, laborious worker who toils without ceasing) with Venus (the Love element, the procreative forces of life) and the Scorpion (Scorpio) the Allegorical Serpent, (sex, temptation, desire to experience, to feel, to live, to produce) all work together through the medium of water and with the energy of Mars (Action) to produce, form, shape and manifest the life in the spiritual seeds of the Creator, God. Taurus, the constellation of the planet Venus is the highest emanation of the Earthy triplicity. Scorpio, the constellation of the planet Mars is the second emanation of the Watery triplicity. So, the Universal Mother with the help of Venus (Love), Scorpio (desire and temptation) and Mars (Action) symbolize the eternal urge to imitate the Creator (God, the Spiritual Sun) striving for diversification, evolution and perfection.

The spiritual seeds (Fire) are planted in Earth (substance) developed in Water (moisture) by Love and Action (Mars) and finally evolve to manifest as Man (the Universal Man, the total of all creation) in Air (infinite space).

The Universal Man being the final results of all action, growth or evolution through Mineral, Vegetable, Animal and Human, The Works Done (good or bad) the manifested results. All are symbolized by Aquarius, the constellation of Man and the planet Uranus, the lowest emanation of the Airy triplicity. These total results also symbolize the accomplishments made by Man with the use of his knowledge and his actions. How far has he evolved in character toward spiritual perfection?

All of this is true of the Universal Man (the total of all manifestation) and true of each Mortal Man, because each Mortal Man is considered a finite or miniature universe containing in essence all of the qualities and attributes of God, the Infinite Creator of all that exists.

The religion of Ancient Egypt was a pure theology based on the laws of Nature as their hierophants saw these laws and forces operate and manifest all the infinite forms of life about them. It took many hundreds of years of close observation and thousands of accurate records to build the foundation of their faith. And hours upon hours of patient study, meditation and silent intuitional prayer to acquire the ability to understand and interpret what they saw and recorded, before they were able to make an accurate and reliable record of their pains taking, laborious, observations.

They only worshiped One God. The others were personified ideas used as a means to instruct others who were unable to understand without having some thing they could see and feel.

Their God was a Spiritual Sun, infinite wisdom, containing all that is, was or ever can be. This Sun was dual, Male and Female (positive and negative, daylight and darkness) and manifested himself, in infinite space, in forms of infinite universes;—the Suns being male or positive and the Planets being female or negative. These universes contained all that is possible (spiritual, mental and material); the planets manifested the life and the suns supplied the vital energy, the spiritual fire of life, for growth and development or evolution. The total of all this manifestation was the Universal Divine Man, God's thoughts in manifestation, or form.

Each mortal man was considered a finite (miniature) universe, containing in minute essence all the qualities and attributes of the infinite creation. And each minute universe was in control of its Lord or Immortal Ego. It was the God given duty for each person to KNOW HIMSELF, correct all faults and deficiences, and rule his kingdom justly.

And notice this;—

The Solar Lion of the Mysteries, the Lion's Paws, the feet of God, the father, the foundation, the roots, are at the bottom.

The Sacred Bull, Apis, the body of the mother, the stalk, the stem, are just above resting on their source.

The Man's Head, the son, the head, knowledge, understanding, the flower, the fruit, the harvest, is resting on its body at the top, to show the results of all previous efforts;—the struggle to live, grow, learn and mature to perfection.

Such is the pattern of life on all planes of existence, Spiritual, Astral (mental), and Physical (material).

FINIS

We believe a great accumulation of valuable ancient manuscripts are stored in a room located in the head of the Sphinx.

CHAPTER XV

THE MYSTERIES OF EROS

Omnia Vincit Veritas

Expressly arranged for the Exterior Circle

of the

Hermetic Brotherhood of Luxor

by T. H. Burgoyne

Private Secretary

PREFACE

In presenting this revelation of the mysteries of man's inner nature to the neophytes belonging to the exterior circle of our venerated order, I am requested to earnestly and solemnly impress upon each and all, personally and individually, the absolute necessity of studying and thoroughly mastering every detail here laid before you. Carefully study out every law, action and principle that may arise in connection with this mighty subject. For it is only by first mastering Nature's alphabet that you can ultimately become Nature's expert scholar, whose trained, disciplined soul can read the Arcane mysteries of the Cosmos, in the clearly written characters traced by the finger of divinity itself all around you.

Make this Arcanum the subject of long, deep, thoughtful study. Commit it to memory, so as to be able to repeat it at pleasure, and when this task is achieved, you will be fully prepared to ascend another step higher in the stairway of Uranias' sacred temple. In conclusion, I must not forget to add that my task throughout has been but that of an amanuensis on one hand and that of a compiler upon the other, for truth is ever the same. "There is nothing new under the sun," saith the wise man;—and so it is with the contents of this Arcanum. Its teachings are as old as the very hills. It is, in fact, but a re-awakened echo from "The Wisdom of the Ages."

Fraternally yours,

J. H. Burgoyne. ⚹.

CHAPTER XV

THE MYSTERIES OF EROS

The Grades of Eros

The grand object of the mysteries of Eros is to build up the individuality of each Acolyte to the end of evolving the latent powers within the human soul. And this must be done by impartial study of ourself. Each person is a miniature universe that he (his Ego) must learn to rule justly. Each individual is a responsible being, working out the problem of his own redemption from the thraldom inherited from ancestry and the dead ages, and forced upon him by external conditions. These mysteries indicate the way, furnish a chart, and bid him square his sails and depart for the shining shores of immortality.

The Arcana of Eros is divided into three separate grades, and for want of better terms can only be described as Formulation, Vitalization and Realization. The first two are triune qualities and contain three principles each. The last is the sum total of the other two and contains but one definition, thus making up a total of seven, which number is the symbol of action and completion of all mundane affairs. Taking the principles as they stand in the order of their relative importance we first come to the grand doctrine and science of Formulation.

I FORMULATION

The three sub-principles of formulation (mental conceptions) are; Formation, Execution and Reception. They each deal specifically upon their own special lines with one of the triune attributes of man's internal nature. Formation is the Creative attribute whereby man imitates deity. Execution is the controlling attribute whereby man receives, conserves or stores up the deific energies and then imitates the laws of his own creation by radiating and projecting this borrowed energy upon the lines, and in the special forms and angles of his own formation (mental creation). Reception is the receptive quality of the soul, whereby man receives and again transmits to the planes below him the grosser forms or the finer essences of the great life-force of the Kosmos, in the exact proportion and ratio of his soul-development and the higher laws of his mentality.

From this it will be seen that Formulation is not only the first principle of man's being, but, that it is at the same time the most vital one with which we have to deal in soul-development.

It is the absolute foundation of all power, knowledge and energy possible to embodied humanity.

Formulation then, in every instance, is to be taken absolutely as the first grand principle to be mastered, studied and applied, in the search for knowledge, and the endeavor to enlarge the scope and range of individual power, mental and psychological, and to this end the following definitions are presented;—(1st. we must know what we desire to accomplish)

a. The Formative (negative) principle, is the quiet, steady, calm, non-turbulent, non-muscular exertion of the human Will. To increase this power and render it practically and magnetically serviceable, a regular daily practice is required. Observe and follow these rules;—

Place a round white card with a black centre against the wall, and gaze at it calmly and steadily one minute, willing at the same time to increase the Attention, Concentration and Abstraction; then slowly turn the eyes to the blank wall; the optical effect will be an apparition of the card, (colors reversed) passing slowly across the line of vision. This may not occur on the first trial, or there may be no more than one or two appear; but after practice the number should and will increase to four, seven or even more. The card may be of any other colors, and the phantoms will be the exact opposite or complementary hue. This exercise is intended to develop the above named power, and its ultimate end and purpose is to enable the acolyte to fix his mind on anything living or dead and will its phantom (in the latter case, itself) to appear. Excellent results may be sooner obtained by using a good magnetic mirror with a white wafer affixed in the centre thereof.

Do not permit the mind to be disturbed or startled if a face or figure appears upon the black-white, magnetic sea of the mirror.

If the acolyte does not possess the necessary nerve for this he had better at once abandon the study of High Magic, which requires heart, courage and persistence for its noblest and most successful culture.

After the card has been in daily use for six months or more it may be abandoned either for the wafered mirror, the head of a brass nail, or better still, three nails; zinc, copper and iron (horseshoe nail) arranged in a triangle whose sides are one inch in length; one end of a fine copper wire should be wound around the three nails and the other held in the left hand while gazing. The effect is magnetic and serves to render the attention more firm, positive and concentrated in a receptive mood. It may and probably will require from two to three years practice before mental conceptions can be successfully substituted for those herein recommended.

One great object for the Neophyte to achieve in this steady practice of formation, is to gradually enable his mind to pierce the Astral light. When the eye is taken from the card, remember that that object has become a thing of the past;—reproducing it again in the phantoms upon the wall is in reality reproducing the past vividly before you. It may be only a few seconds of time, still no matter how brief, it is still the past, and careful daily practice will enable the Neophyte to become more and more potent in this realm of Psychology, and render it possible for him to reproduce instantly any object or scene of his experience, no matter how remote. This will gradually lead the soul into the state of not only reading and producing its own past experience, but of delineating the past history of any other object or person in all its original reality, through the law of psychometry. Therefore, simple as this principle of Formation may seem, it is the first stepping stone in the path of the soul's ultimate state of perfection, which is that of the real Master of Mysteries, the exalted Adept.

b. The executive is the second principle, and is purely volitional (positive). It is the projecting, ordering, commanding and mentally enforcing the behests of Desire and Will;—to say, think, feel and ordain a thing to be or an action to occur, and as such, is the opposite pole of the first principle, Formation. It is the must and shall be idea in action, the positive, executive force of the human soul, without a proper culture and activity of which no great thing, whether within or without the path of White Magic, can be accomplished. It is the blessing or cursing energy of the soul and is at once the grandest

and most terrible force, alike potent for good or evil. Its action
is periodical, its orbit elliptical and its effect magnetic; therefore,
what it takes from you it always returns with interest;—if good,
then good; if evil, then added evil; so beware.

Great care must be taken that there is no other emotion or action
going on in the mind during the executive instant, for this ordaining
power, (especially after the exercise of the Formative), leaps from
the soul like a flash of vivid lighting, traversing space and centering
on its object though oceans flow between, or vast spaces divide; yet
its period of activity and duration never exceeds three to seven seconds of earthly time.

c. The third or Receptive principle consists in placing one's
self in a receptive position, state, frame of body, mind and feeling,
to receive the message. It is the most important and difficult of the
three great principles, and its results;—especially in affectional lines;
correspond (good attracts good, evil attracts more evil). To exert it
successfully requires a fair development of attention, concentration
and abstraction, in addition to the exercise of the Formative and Executive principles, not merely as regards any special object or power
to be sought, but to induce the Receptive condition itself. When we
strike or sustain a blow we pose the body, hands, face, eyes, nostrils
and mouth; even so is the same rule imperative in the higher or su-
perphysical, metaphysical, mental and ethereal regions of our vast
being, and it must be enforced in order to reach the sublimest of all
receptive powers. There is no Magic save in Formation, Execution
and Reception; and their foundation is Love.

To illustrate our meaning, let us say for example, air and heat
rush in to fill a vacuum, and there can be no vacuum if anything is
there. Similarly one cannot wholly either notice, wish for, will, decree,
or receive the full measure of anything sought, or power desired,
or the entire weight of any mental or metaphysical desideratum, if
half or more of the mind is already occupied by something else
which receives a proportion of its attention and of the heart's desire.
The vacuum is created by a sincere desire to receive what is sought.

This principle requires the entire devotion, absorption and concentration of all the inner being. When a thing is to be done, an
Energy (individual in both senses), hierarchy or special power is to
be invoked and brought down from the aerial kingdoms of the spaces,

or evolved and called up from within, the mind must not only be brought to wholly bear upon the reception thereof, but room within the Odyllic sphere must be provided for the expected visitor and the entire attention of the soul be withdrawn and vacated, except for that special thing, gift, energy or power then sought through the mysteries of Eros.

This road is a royal one; the weak minded, blind or credulous can never travel its imperial path, because the higher powers only have an affinity with those capable of appreciating them; they never coalesce with starvling souls, and never at all, unless the laws of their evocation, development, operation and evolution, are earnestly, calmly, steadily, persistently followed and implicitly obeyed.

II VITALIZATION

The second of the three great principles of the triune soul is Vitalization, which means life giving. Everything is vitalized in exact proportion to the capacity of reception and transmission. Every spirit atom or Divine Ego, is in reality a central point or Focus of Deity for the transmission of life.

The soul Monad projected into matter, in order to evolve the latent attributes of the divine spirit, is supplied incessantly from its own state and center with the life force required, and it in return transmits it to planes and states still lower than itself, involuntarily, in most instances.

Everything, from the highest Arch-Angelhood to the cold granite rock and dense veins of mineral, is in a state of reception and transmission. That all human beings in the natural state are mediumistic (except avaricious misers), some in excess of others, must, to be in accord with the laws herein revealed, appear perfectly plain, especially so, when we comprehend the relationship of humanity to Deity. In a similar manner all material substances are mediumistic in this sense of the term, viz.; in the degree in which they are capable of receiving and transmitting Force. In this connection, Hermetic Science teaches, that active spirit inheres in every grade of matter as the instigator of life, force and motion, being an attendant upon the ethereal forces that permeate all worlds and every atom of space. For in proportion to the refinement of substance is the sphere vitalized by spirit.

In the brain and nervous system of the human being the Climax of Material Vitalization is reached, hence as the Neophyte by training gradually builds up his individuality, and refines his physical organism by throwing off the grosser particles and replacing them with more ethereal ones, he becomes capable of receiving, retaining and transmitting the finer and more potential essences of the Astral Light; consequently his will is correspondingly potent within the realms of White Magic.

Taken in a general sense Vitalization may be divided into three separate sections, viz; Inspiration, Exspiration and Breathing. The latter as the most external embraces the two former. Considered separately, we have first, Inspiration

> "The simple senses crowned his Head,
> 'Omega, thou art Lord', they said."

> "Who forged that other influence
> That heat of inward evidence?"   Tennyson.

The discriminating student will not fail to note much significance in the four lines quoted above. The sentiment of the first couplet is declarative, affirmative, positive, assertive, active, or briefly, Male. The second couplet is equally distinctive in its sentiment, but the diametrical opposite, being that of inquiry, solicitation, invitation, negation, or Female.

Considered relatively they are polar opposites. They also possess a broad generalization, or, more properly, a classification of the world's creeds and doctrines upon inspiration, its sources and rank. One class claiming that inspiration is of the senses and intellect; another, that it is external to the senses and intellect. Hermetic science does not join in alliance with either one of the two doctrines as against the other, but teaches that both are the complimentary halves of a complete truth; expressed otherwise, a unity under two modes of action. When the mode of action is considered, duality stands squarely before us. Indeed, consciousness itself is due to the ebb and flow of the energies that pertain to duality. Inspiration means in-breathing. We inspire the essences and forces of the One Life according to our refinement of material structure and adaptation for receiving it.

The Gates of Heaven open inwardly; so does inspiration, and when we have in-breathed and replenished the body, soul and spirit, the action becomes polarized, reaction sets in, and we throw off and transmit all that our system is unable to neutralize or assimilate. This brings us to the second section of our subject, namely, Exspiration.

EXSPIRATION

Exspiration means out-breathing, out-flowing thoughts, or expulsion of any fluidic substance or essence. It also takes the meaning of loss or extinguishment, and herein stands as the antithesis of inspiration, which is so significant of cumulation and gain. When we further consider that the framers of our linguistic symbols spoke of breath, and air or wind, as being or containing the intrinsic Potencies, the inspiration and exspiration of this kind, meant flatly, either gain or loss of power. Exspiration is the emission, loss or expenditure of power. The loss or absence of power leaves behind it the attribute or correlative state, which we call coldness. It is not mere verbal fancy to speak of the heat and fires of inspiration, for herein we have a veritable truth. Inspiration and Exspiration are related as the Vishnu and Siva, preserver and destroyer in oriental religion.

It has been said that no man can serve two masters; but herein is a paradox, for it is plain that we do seventy times every minute transfer our subserviency from one to the other of these two sovereigns; one brings us emancipation and the other takes it away. The pulse of the heart and the exspiration of spirit is our inspiration, while we expire to lower forms of life. "Tantalus, thou art living still." But the philosopher, looking beyond the scope of the present times, sees therein the law of faithful compensation and the equipoise of beneficence, for we are not privileged to reap unless we likewise sow. It is also an exposition of that law, "Give all thou hast of breath, or power, or life, in just duty and lawful motive; expire honestly the corrupted or contaminated matter, and you shall instantly be filled with the celestial fire and become refined." Too much inspiration causes levitation, too much exspiration, gravitation.

We now come to the realization of these two sections, the actuality of both inspiration and exspiration, and which may be totalized as Breathing.

BREATHING

There are two results of breathing; the first is from the inspiration of common atmosphere which sustains the life of matter, sensation. The second result is from the inspiration of the magnetic, electric, more ethereal particles of the air, which support the life of soul and emotion; the higher, inner, deeper part of man which concerns itself about infinite and eternal interests. The first gives force, the second generates power. It is possible to fill the lungs, therefore the brain, with this last, sifted from the first, and thus the soul, with ascensive inclination and ability, with the loftier kind of trance-power, known as the "Sacred Sleep of Sialam," in which the soul bids defiance to all barriers which, awake, asleep, or in the mesmeric states, limit and bound it; with that grand flight-power whereby it can reach infinite altitudes and sweep with masterly vision the realm of stellar galaxies; that Sleep of Sialam, in which man may gain whatsoever of knowledge and power he wills, provided it lies within his soul's capacity of comprehending and using.

By slowly, regularly breathing, two things occur; to give strength and power. First, a gain of vitality, therefore, physical life. The organs instantly extract the *vif* of the air and discharge their accumulated load. The exhalent movement is always the longer in natural breathing; but, if you wish to gain power and have more ethereal than physical life, the heaving of the chest should be regular and its inspirations and exspirations of equal duration to obtain a more harmonious influence and the slow breathing must go on from ten to twenty minutes at a time. Fix some desired object in the mind and the ethereal air will be retained in the lungs, brain and nerves until sufficient reserve force is gained to add new power, thus enabling the soul to subdue sense and affording the pure intellect ability to take lofty, prolonged, and heaven-sublimed flights into the Empyrean, or, in any direction fancy or inclination prompts or necessity suggests.

This is one of the most potential powers within the human soul.

The term AETH signifies that finer essence which the soul breathes; it fills the spaces, cushions the worlds and penetrates the outer air just as odors do. It is inhaled by Aethereal beings precisely as we of earth inhale the influence of matter in its grosser and lower forms. No real divine or celestial energy can be evolved until, by patient and continued effort, the Neophyte learns to inhale the Aether while the mind is firmly fixed upon what is in and of it. Thereby he contacts the essence of power and the denizens of the ethereal and far-off spaces. Thus doing will he breathe the elements which generate power in the Human soul.

Remember, O Neophyte, that Goodness alone is Power, Silence is Strength, Will regaineth Omnipotentence, and Love lieth at the foundation of all.

These forces should never be trifled with; should never be brought into action for any mere worldly or temporal motives; because their sphere of action pertains only to the highest and most interior states that it is possible for embodied man to penetrate.

Note;—The student should extend this philosophy of exspiration and inspiration to his body griefs and captious irritants of every kind. Expire them all, cast them out, and make room for better company, which will flow in like a festive troop if you will make room and extend them a cordial invitation. Mean thoughts, passions and low ideals, have killed thousands. You cannot afford to entertain such guests. Therefore, expire them with your next breath, and bid them an eternal farewell.   T.H.B.

III REALIZATION

All centers, Spheres, Potencies, Hierarchies, and Brotherhoods, in fact, all things on earth externalized, have their orbits and periods. In like manner, all conceivable powers, qualities and energies in the spaces, have the same. There are times when they are, and are not, contactible, and it is very difficult, if not impossible, for any-one living in domestic turmoil to contact them at all, save through the exercise of a resolute, unbending will, and perfect indifference to the surrounding inharmony; but there are orders of beings, invisible to material eyes, who were of earth once, and others who have never been ultimated on, nor incarnated within this external plane of objective life who understand anything and everything of which man can conceive; who possess every species of knowledge, and who respond to the desire and invocation of those who follow the same lines of thought and feeling, who belong to the same state of intelligence, or who voluntarily place themselves under the essential conditions of rapport and contact.

The Neophyte must be careful to divest the mind of all but the subject in hand; never seek for two dissimilar objects at the same time, or within seven clear days between the operations, every one of which should be prepared for with a full heart by fastings, ablutions and soul aspiration. Study these laws thoroughly nor forget this caution; nothing can be done except through Law, Order, Rule and a clear, definite comprehension of the underlying principles set forth herein, and above all, a perfect Formulation of the objects desired. But before proceeding further it is advisable to consider one or two points, which, in the end, will be found to be of great service to the thinking student of the Philosophy now taught. There is no accident, nor any such thing as Chance in this life or the worlds beyond; all external things and events are the results of internal causes, and there are rules by which they can be forecasted and anticipated by contacting the intelligences of that sphere. We do not mean by this, that all human events and occurrences are foreseen by those who were once denizens of the world we inhabit, and who for redemptive or other ends may reveal many things to their worthy proteges; but we mean that within this universe, there is a great central source of intelligence, power, presence and energy, which necessarily knows all that was, is, and is to be. This central power must be environed by colossal mental energies, potentialities in knowledge, only second to its Supreme Self; nor do we conceive such potencies to be ascended human beings, who once dwelt in physical bodies, lived, died and rose again. There are electrical, ethereal, non-material universes, far grander, vaster and more magnificent than this of ours with all its amazing splendors, its myriad galaxies and rain-storms of starry systems; with all its inconceivable distances, and stretch of fathomless eternities, than this of ours is superior to an anthill. There are Hierarchies, legions of them, Potencies, Powers, and Intelligencies, not of human material genesis, before whose amazing sweep of mind the grandest intellect earth ever has or can produce is as a pebble to a mountain range, a tiny dewdrop to the mighty rush of oceans' waters, a gentle shower to a tempest of rain, a zephyr to the raging typhoon on its devastating march o'er land and sea.

These beings are the arbiters of the destinies of the worlds, and the Planetary Angels, originators of the grand drama of external life.

The capacity of Deity is boundless; that of man is limited, and is either vast or contracted in strict accordance with the relative ratio of his soul development and independence of mere bodily sense, personal or material bias. Perfect development means perfect at-one-ment; this atonement is the sacrifice of the lower nature upon the cross of purification and the evolution of the true Christ within; the real Christian, beyond all creed, exists only in the truly perfected man. One so developed can place himself en-rapport with the centers of celestial life, traverse the spaces, and penetrate the grand arcana of the universe itself.

Man has not omniscience, but has much penetration; he is not omnipotent, yet possesses enormous latent powers; he cannot be omni-present, but is capable of Ubique; that is, of being mentally and spir-itually in many places and scenes at the same time. A million photo-graphic instruments will instantly chain a million shadows or images of any object because all surrounding space is filled with millions of such prototypes, given off by everything continually; this is even more true of the soul than of the body, and this fact brings us face to face with the sublime mystery of Projection and that of its opposite, Soul-attraction.

Projection means the sending, forcing, compelling of the astral form, (double or soul symbol) to appear wherever the will may com-mand through the three principles of Formulation.

Attraction is the exercise of the same power in the opposite di-rection, to compel the apparition of another. Wherever the Neophyte has sufficient steady will-force to decree his presence, he may compel the appearance of whatever phantom or intelligence he chooses, and may act with enormous force upon whom he desires.

OBSERVE;—Formulation can be excited from two planes; 1st. from pure intellect, cold and joyless, which is its negative force or plane; and 2nd. from the heart, the soul-emotional, or love-plane, which is its positive point of action. Execution is always masculine, positive, ordering, commanding, electric—of the brain alone. Recep-tion requires instantaneous transition from the masculine brain to the tender, soft, loving, emotional side of nature.

Woman is the receptive and Man the executive force. He im-parts, she receives; so also the intellect of man acts on imperative principles, her love on receptive ones; this is the law.

All good works begin and end with devout aspirations, and posing to receive the boon craved, while desires of an opposite nature begin with, and end on, opposite principles. In all matters connected with the punishment of wrong, the protection of the weak, and imparting power, health and prosperity to others, Execution terminates the formula, invariably. In actual practice the Neophyte must first remember that the party or person to be frustrated must be present, either in person or apparitional presence, which latter can be achieved by the process of Formulation; this force must be contained until the apparitional image or images stand out clearly defined before the operator; then think that which is required to be done and formulate it just as clearly; at this point the Executive force must be projected on its orbit. But it must never be forgotten or overlooked, that this executive force is to be retained within the grasp of the operator during the climax of the formulative moment, and never projected until the soul is full to overflowing, or it will fail to reach its object, and, having traversed its orbit, recoil upon the operator and produce inharmony.

Let us solemnly impress upon each and every Neophyte the fearful dangers that will overtake him should he ever attempt to use these powers for evil purposes or the injury of others; therefore, be warned and rather suffer injustice than retaliate with vengeance.

Note;—In repelling any evil influence that is or may be directed against him, the Neophyte must use the powers of Execution wisely, not with vengeance, but with cold, withering, lofty contempt, desiring neither vengeance on the one hand nor giving mercy on the other. It is that state of mind which is calm, cold, heartless and indifferent to all save self-protection; it is a state of stern, unbending justice, and extremely difficult to be obtained.   T.H.B.

PSYCHICAL CULTURE

A brief System of Soul Development, with Rules for Practical Occult Training, specially adapted to the Natural Requirements of the Western Members of the Exterior Circle of The Hermetic Brotherhood of Luxor.

INTRODUCTION

The primary law to be remembered in all and every species of occult training, is that of equilibrium. The scientific evolution of the latent powers of the human soul is just as much the result of methodical procedure and constant application as the training and education of the young. No sudden results can naturally be expected. If there are, they are premature and abnormal, and instead of cultivating them, they must be retarded, since the perfect harmony of equilibrium has been violently disturbed.

In the cultivation of the psychical powers and attributes of the soul, ever remember that there must be the seed time and the maturing period before the season of reaping arrives, when we can expect to gather in the spiritual fruits of our laborious toil and industry.

The Neophyte must, first of all, thoroughly understand what he is about, and not set blindly to work. He must have a perfect conception of what spiritual training and discipline is, before he makes any attempt in its actual practice, to enable him to arrive at a fairly correct idea of this extremely important subject. The following brief but significant hints can be very profitably meditated upon.

Occult training, or Psychical culture means, primarily, the enfranchisement of the soul. Secondly, it means the cultivation and practical utilization of the spiritual senses of the soul. And lastly, it means the complete subjugation of every animal passion, principle and desire within us, to the undisputed harmonious control of the divine selfhood.

Commit these facts well to memory, and also remember, that vice, habit and passion, or other inharmonious traits of character, must be conquered. Until this is accomplished we are but the helpless mediums of matter. It is not the actual, external indulgence in any particular practices that constitute the real vice, but it is the power, force and magnetic control which this habit or practice gains over the inner self, that constitutes the actual transgression against the higher laws of our being.

Having briefly outlined the broad principle of Psychical culture, it is now only necessary to add a few words of warning. No practice, whether it be that of using tobacco immoderately, drinking intoxicants, or any other petty vice, must be checked immediately, but slowly, gradually, in fact, almost imperceptibly. A sudden suspension means a sudden reaction, and above everything else, psychical culture requires quiet repose, equilibrium. No man can take a sudden leap from Hades to Heaven. It is as well he cannot, because he would be out of place and worse off than when in his previously congenial hell, consequently, it is impossible to jump from the planes of selfish sensual desire, into the realm of spiritual light in a single day, week, month or year. It is a process of gradual growth;—first, the seed time, then the maturing period, lastly, the spiritual harvest of heavenly fruit. Remember this and your spiritual discipline will be conducted wisely, worthily and well.

RULES FOR OCCULT TRAINING

1st. The Neophyte must abstain from smoking, the use of intoxicants, flesh eating, etc. The diet must be pure, wholesome, and be strictly vegetarian in nature.

2nd. Each morning, or as often as possible, the Neophyte must take a cold or tepid bath, according as the natural constitution is robust or delicate. When the bath is not convenient, the body must be well rubbed with a coarse, wet towel.

3rd. During the day, whether engaged in business or otherwise, there must be a strong, systematic effort made to check the slightest evil thought, word or deed, and gossip, under all circumstances, must be completely prohibited. In fact, the Neophyte, while pleasantly performing the necessary duties of life, must cultivate a quiet, calm, reserved, self-possessed state of mind, and endeavor to his utmost to hold in check grief, joy, surprise, pleasure or pain; for be it remembered that the passions and sensations of the body are each and all but petty, subordinate states, or in other words, centers of occult force which ever strive to usurp the imperial rule of the true monarch, the human Will. The vast majority of mankind are but mere slaves of their predispositions and earthly passions, and seem to the true occultist like an empire divided into innumerable small states, each of which has a ruling prince of its own, powerful enough to totally ignore any command of his liege lord whenever it suits his pleasure to object. Until the body is brought under the command of the Will and stands in absolute subjection to the soul, occult progress, except in degrees, is simply impossible; and this is the greatest barrier with which the Neophyte has to grapple, viz.; SELF;—"first conquer thyself, and then, but not till then, mayest thou hope to conquer the forces of Nature," is the advice of our revered Grand Master, M. Theon.

4th. When the Neophyte has advanced a few degrees on the path toward self-control, active training should commence immediately after the morning ablution, and in the evening practice with the mirror, or crystal meditation which follows the card practice.

5th. When convenient obtain some of the dhoop insense such as is used in the Hindu temples. Place the mirror or crystal in position, and, sitting in a passive state of mind, gaze into the center or focus, repeating this incantation every two or three minutes; "My soul is one with the Universe, and my Spirit an emanation from God."

Then let the mind meditate upon these mystic words, and at the same time the spiritual soul-sight will slowly but surely penetrate the Astral light collected from the eyes of the Neophyte upon the sensitive, magnetic surface of the mirror. The mind should be kept as spiritual as possible during the practice, and all worldly objects banished.

6th. The evening practice is very different from the above. The Neophyte should sit in an easy chair or recline upon a couch in the most easy position, and then gaze upon the card or wafered mirror, (see the first of this chapter), and commence to formulate mental or metaphysical objects, and then try to project them externally upon the wall or ceiling. He may also find much benefit from a psychic point of view, if he tries to reproduce any of the objects seen during the day. This is the grand secret of penetrating the Astral light of the past. By secret, we mean that this is the commencement of the pathway that leads to the secrets of the Astral light, itself. Remember that one can neither make a talisman nor make the powers of a magic spell for good or evil until he becomes the complete master of the phase, viz.; "Formulation." The best time generally for such practice in the evening, is twilight or near midnight, and at sunrise (just before) for the morning meditation.

7th. And lastly, the moral tone of the Neophyte's life must be pure, spotless and unsullied by selfish desires. Especially must all sexual relations be carefully guarded, and only participated in after due thought and careful study of desires and intentions. It is this very fatal mistake of sex that has ruined thousands of otherwise promising aspirants for occult initiation.

CONCLUDING NOTE

The awful list of powers, attributes and forces set forth in the works of P. B. Randolph, as attainable by the actual use of the sexual force, is a terrible snare. It was this fatal mistake that ruined the unfortunate, misguided Randolph himself. Therefore, remember, if you value your soul's immortality, that evil powers can be so gained, but those who gain them are forever lost. It is the true way to Voudooism and Black Magic. SO BEWARE how you play with the infernal laws which rule the realms of animal nature and outer darkness.

CPSIA information can be obtained at www.ICGtesting.com
Printed in the USA
BVOW02s0044121015

421898BV00001B/189/P